Aha! Moments:
When Intellect and Intuition Collide

How to Make Better Decisions
Using the Power of
Aha! Moments

Inspired Leap

Aha! Moments: When Intellect and Intuition Collide
How to Make Better Decisions Using the Power of Aha! Moments
By Dianna Amorde

Copyeditor and Index: Christine Frank, www.ChristineFrank.com
Cover and Interior design: Toolbox Creative, www.ToolboxCreative.com

"The Journey" from Dream Work by Mary Oliver. Copyright © 1986 by Mary Oliver. Used by permission of Grove/Atlantic, Inc.

Library of Congress Cataloguing-in-Publications Data
Library of Congress Control Number: 2009923841

Amorde, Dianna.
Aha! moments : when intellect & intuition collide :
how to make better decisions using the power of aha!
moments / Dianna Amorde. -- 1st ed.
p. cm.
Includes bibliographical references and index.
LCCN 2009923841
ISBN-13: 978-0981932606
ISBN-10: 0981932606

1. Intuition. 2. Insight. 3. Decision making.
I. Title.

BF315.5.A46 2009 153.4'4
QBI09-600019

For my brother David

Witnessing your ability "to accept the things I cannot change"
leaves me in awe and honored to call you brother.
May you, Lisa, Michelle, Matthew, and Eric find the meaning
and hidden gifts in the challenges you face.

Table of Contents

Introduction

The title *Aha! Moments: When Intellect and Intuition Collide* describes the transformation of my life. For when I finally acknowledged the power of my intuition and enabled it to collide with and often override my intellect, my life took a sharp turn in the direction of a new career that rewards me daily.

Looking back, I can see that over the years I slowly but surely began to devalue, and then ignore, what my intuition was telling me. I was determined to get to the top of the corporate ladder in the traditional way, by developing and emphasizing my logical, analytical, and strategic thinking abilities. To that end, I worked hard and generated mostly A's in college. And, using my successes in work, academics, and school activities, I went off to Harvard Business School to further develop my abilities to think and lead effectively.

But my professors never taught me to develop, access, and trust my own inner wisdom. I don't know about you, but I was taught to trust the data before trusting myself. In hindsight, this seems extraordinarily narrow-minded, as time and again, both professional and personal decisions involved a mix of conflicting data, expert opinions, and gut reaction. Yet educational institutions and the business world sweep under the rug the role that intuition must play in any decision in order to have it be effective. And we aren't given any language to help articulate intelligently why something does or doesn't feel right, without fear of appearing foolish or being ridiculed for our feelings.

When I look back on the best decisions I ever made as a manager, they always involved a strong gut feel that it was the right decision. That gut feeling gave me the confidence to argue my case in front of my managers—sometimes passionately—for my recommended plan of action. And the worst decisions always came when I'd lost my confidence and ignored what my intuition was telling me—dismissing my intuitive unease as an upset stomach, being tired, or not having enough knowledge about the topic being discussed.

After twenty years in the corporate world, I left it as a burned-out workaholic with no confidence in my ability to generate a creative idea or make an effective decision. By not understanding and ultimately denying my intuitive gifts, I'd cut myself off from a vital part of my intelligence and strengths. I was a shell of myself and my health reflected it. I spent months trying to figure out what went wrong.

The more I learned about the way leading-edge scientists and thinkers now theorize how we and the world work and interact with each other, the more I realized the vital importance intuition plays in generating the ideas and optimal decisions that take us in the direction we're called to go. We make it so hard on ourselves when we deny the wisdom our intuitive side offers us at any given moment.

That's what I did. I wore my self out mentally, physically, emotionally, and spiritually because I didn't understand what my gifts were and how best to use them in a corporate setting. The more I tried to fit in, the more exhausted I became. I was trying to deliver results without using the best of me. Through a series of aha! moments, I slowly but surely realized that the corporate path was no longer a good fit for me.

But the knowledge that many others were leaving companies drained without understanding why, and many more were simply existing at work, one day to the next, too exhausted and afraid to make a leap in a new direction, galvanized me to create Inspired Leap Consulting. So, despite the concerns of peers who wondered why I was walking away from a clearly mapped out and lucrative career path for something so abstract, I launched Inspired Leap in 2003. While some still consider intuition a 'soft' topic, unworthy of focus by someone with a Harvard MBA, I find more and more people who are awakening to the understanding that intuition is a form of intelligence and even knowing that is critical to making the optimal decision in any situation, even in a corporate office.

With the world seemingly spinning faster and faster, requiring more and more rapid decisions, we're all faced with many moments in our days when we must make a 'snap' decision, with access to limited, if any, data. Even if we are blessed to have all of the data or knowledge we'd like at our fingertips, many times the data are conflicting. What do we do then? Ultimately, the decision resides with us.

No decision tree analysis, expert advice, or even psychic prognostication can make a decision about your work or your life better than you. You are far more brilliant and powerful than you think. It's time to access and use that wisdom and power.

I chose to write this book specifically about aha! moments, rather than hunches, gut feelings, or intuition in general because of how powerful they are. The number one question I'm asked about intuition is, 'How do I know it's really intuition? What if it's just wishful thinking on my part or fear of change?' The beauty of aha! moments is that they deliver a strong feeling of knowing with the information or clarity we need, so we *know* the information we've received is worthy to use in guiding us in all of our decisions.

The more I explored the possible sources of both the physical experience of aha! moments and the wisdom they deliver, I realized that these seemingly miraculous moments provide a wealth of insight into how to maximize the resources available to us at any given moment. With this wisdom in hand, each of us can make the optimal decision for ourselves, our families, our teams, or our companies every time we're faced with an important decision.

My objective is to inspire you to see yourself, how you interact with this amazing world we live in, and how you think of aha! moments and intuition in a whole new way. And, once you shift your thinking, I intend to inspire you to confidently make some bold decisions and take some inspired leaps. Most of us have at least one or two decisions we've put off making because we've been afraid of what comes next. What decisions do you need to make?

So read on to be inspired to cultivate more aha! moments, to trust their wisdom, and to confidently make better decisions....

Chapter One **Aha!**

Karen* was stuck. She'd been out of a job for over six months and was
beginning to panic. She had no energy left for doing the groundwork
for gaining interviews, let alone acting confident in an interview, even if
she were to obtain one.

Looking to find clarity about what to do to find a job, Karen used a
letter-writing technique for accessing the intelligence stored within her
nonconscious (or subconscious) mind and her soul's higher wisdom to
help her move forward on her job search. At the end of the workshop
Karen attended, I took all of the letters and mailed them to the attendees. Karen anxiously awaited the answer she requested (directed by her
to come from her nonconscious mind within forty-eight hours of writing the letter).

Two days after the workshop, Karen walked out to her mailbox
to get her mail. As she glanced at the stack of mail, she saw the letter
she'd written two nights before. It was depressing to realize that she still
had no answer—even her nonconscious mind was letting her down!
"Perhaps," she thought, "I just haven't paid enough attention—maybe I
received an intuitive message or sign and missed it."

. . . .
* Unless otherwise noted, names have been changed and the summary of the experience is in my
words based on what I witnessed or learned from the client in an e-mail.

As Karen flipped through the rest of her mail, she paused to look at the magazine that had arrived. She gasped as she studied the picture. Aha! There was her answer. She briskly walked back into her home, knowing with confidence and clarity what her next step in her job search should be.

In Karen's case, writing a letter to her nonconscious mind enabled her to heighten her awareness of her intuition. The act of writing down her question also signaled to her Higher Self* or soul that she was ready to acknowledge what her Higher Self had likely known all along, but was hidden and seemingly unreachable beneath the anxiety of too many choices and too much in the way of information, expertise, and outside opinions.

When Karen first glanced at the magazine cover and saw the photograph of the city of Dallas, Texas, she told me the colors of the photo were especially vibrant and seemed to jump out at her. At that moment, everything fell into place internally. She immediately realized that she didn't want to look for a job in Austin, Texas where she'd lost her job and currently lived. She wanted to move back to Dallas where her family was. Once she acknowledged this personal truth, things started happening. Karen found the energy to update her resume with needed changes, her phone started ringing with opportunities, and soon Karen was headed to Dallas for interviews.

Karen experienced the lightning bolt of knowing and clarity that many people describe as an aha! moment or an epiphany.

What Is an Aha! Moment?

We all know it when we experience it. The classic image of the light bulb flashing on above a person's head while they exclaim, 'aha!' says

----

* If the term 'Higher Self' is new to you, think of it as representing the wisest part of you, the part closest to the Divine (however you define it) and similar to the meaning of soul or spirit. If you believe in reincarnation, then the Higher Self would be the part of you that continues after each lifetime.

it all: suddenly the answer or next step is illuminated and the person wonders why she hadn't thought of this obvious idea before. Similar to an epiphany, an aha! moment literally feels like a sudden zap of insight or intuition has come down from above to give us the clarity we so desperately need.

While many people describe an epiphany the same way they do an aha! moment, I like to think of an epiphany as an intense or supercharged aha! experience. It delivers a dramatic transformational insight. The wisdom is so profound that your life is changed forever. Whether you want to call it an epiphany or an aha! moment, we're simply talking about the range of clarity or insight. You'll know you've had one of these divine moments when you experience the bliss of peace, clarity, and confidence. All doubt, worry, and fear drops away—if only for a moment—and a brilliant idea, *the* answer, or a solid next step for a project comes to you.

As the chart on the following page indicates, your aha! moment is a powerful form of intuition because the clarity comes without your actively thinking about it. You aren't using any logic, analysis, or deductive reasoning. You simply *experience* a leap in knowing or understanding without any conscious reasoning to arrive at that knowing. As Albert Einstein is reputed to have said about these leaps in consciousness, "The answer comes to you and you don't know how or why."

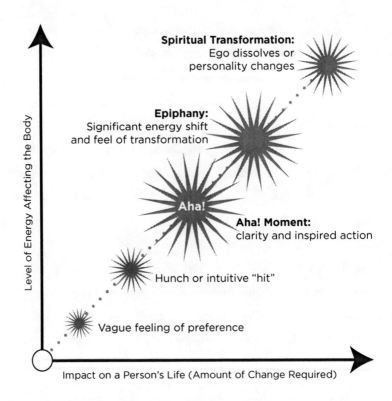

Bigger Is Not Always Better

Once you move beyond a guess, all forms of intuitive knowing are valid and worth following up on. Many of us were raised in a culture that encouraged 'bigger is better' thinking, so we might be inclined to assume aha! moments are superior to hunches, epiphanies are better than aha! moments, and those dramatic spiritual transformations are the 'best' way to receive intuitive guidance. If that describes your typical line of reasoning, consider the following: the bigger the aha! or epiphany, the bigger the immediate effect on you and your life. So a series of subtle hunches can be a lot easier to handle than a big, life-changing epiphany. And consider the possibility that the only reason a dramatic epiphany is needed is that you won't pay attention to the hunches and aha! moments that keep coming your way.

In order to regularly operate from the clarity that aha! experiences bring and avoid dramatic shifts in your energy and your life, all you need to do is open up to your intuitive intelligence and pay attention to the way it 'speaks' to you.

Access Aha! Moments: Use Your Intuitive Intelligence

The phrase *intuitive intelligence* is meant to convey the intelligent processing that goes on within the mind, even if hidden, when we access our intuition. Some people mistakenly associate intuition with any thought or idea that isn't part of a conscious thinking process, including random guesses. True intuition—intuitive *intelligence*—has nothing to do with guessing or 'shooting from the hip' decision-making.

My favorite definition for intuition is "a way of knowing without the conscious use of reasoning."[1] The key words are *knowing, conscious,* and *reasoning.* Your conscious mind does not 'know' how it knows what it knows, but your nonconscious mind has done its work and sends a signal telling you via a hunch, gut feeling, or other sensation that you've got the *right* answer. If it's using stored data, for example, it might be saying "We've seen this situation before, in fact many times before, so pick door number three or supplier X or job applicant Z," and so on.

A Note on Subconscious versus Nonconscious:

For many years, most of us have associated that hidden part of our mind with the term 'subconscious.' However, as we learn more about this very powerful part of ourselves, it has become clear that there's nothing 'sub' about it. So some scientists are referring to this vast area of your mind as either 'unconscious' or 'nonconscious.'[2]

I prefer to say 'nonconscious mind' to refer to the thinking or processing part of our brain that we have no conscious access to. 'Unconscious' makes me think of what happens if you faint or 'lose consciousness.' Use the term that works best for you. Just make sure you regularly remind yourself how powerful this part of you truly is.

We have a strong bias, particularly in the U.S., of assuming that attempting to rationally and logically think our way through to an answer—many times via sifting through mounds of data and expert opinion—is a superior way, if not the only way, to make a decision. I strongly disagree and throughout this book will show you why. No system of decision-making is foolproof, but I'd like you to consider the possibility that you have an inner guidance system that is far more brilliant than you think.

Your most powerful way of confidently accessing this inner guidance system is via aha! moments and your intuitive intelligence.

Exercise Your Right Brain For More Aha's

Research indicates that intuition or this 'way of knowing' is the way the right hemisphere of your brain processes or receives information. Your left hemisphere, on the other hand, likes to 'think' and process information logically and analytically. When people talk about 'getting out of your head and into your heart,' they're really saying 'get out of your left brain and into your right brain.'

A number of books have come out in the last few years explaining the importance of and need for development of the right hemisphere of the brain.[3] Thankfully, we are now beginning to understand that traditional education and training that focus almost exclusively on the left hemisphere's logical, analytical, verbal way of processing information is not optimal. In order to achieve the greatness we are all capable of, we must also actively develop and engage the abilities of the right hemisphere of the brain, the intuitive, holistic, and visual way of processing information.

Differences in Processing Information Between the Left and Right Hemispheres of the Brain

Characteristics of the LEFT Hemisphere	Characteristics of the RIGHT Hemisphere
Logical	Intuitive
Analytical	Nonlinear
Verbal	Visual
Sequential	Holistic
Tends to dominate right hemisphere	Tends to let left hemisphere lead
Reductive in thinking (wants to get to one right answer)	Inclusive in thinking (happy to keep juggling numerous possible solutions)
Corresponds to right side of body	Corresponds to left side of body
Men tend to be more left-brain dominant	**Women tend to be more right-brain dominant**

One note of caution: As neuroscientists are quick to point out, all of this talk about left brain versus right brain can lead you to think you have two brains that operate separately. This is not true. Studies show that both hemispheres work together, but have distinct roles in processing information. For example, while the left hemisphere is the dominant player in your verbal abilities, the right hemisphere has been shown to lead the way in interpreting the vocal tone of spoken language.[4]

Yet, as you'll see below, our two hemispheres do seem to have unique personalities and each of us has more of a preference (or comfort level?) for one hemisphere's point of view.

In her fascinating and inspiring book, *My Stroke of Insight*, Jill Bolte Taylor, Ph.D., a brain anatomist, takes us on a riveting ride through her personal experience of suffering a severe stroke at the age of thirty-five and her nearly nine years of recovery. Much of the recovery period was devoted to re-developing the left hemisphere of her brain, which was heavily damaged, if not destroyed, by the stroke. Yet in the process of working so hard to recover her left-brain thinking and processing abilities, Taylor came to develop a previously unimagined (pre-stroke) reverence for the talents and perspective of her right brain.

Taylor explains the value, beauty, and power of the right hemisphere and how it connects us to all that is. While she went to great lengths to regain access to the skills of her left hemisphere, Taylor admits she did so cautiously, as she came to cherish the experience of viewing the world from a right-brain perspective:

> My right mind character is adventurous, celebrative of abundance, and socially adept. It is sensitive to nonverbal communication, empathetic, and accurately decodes emotion. My right mind is open to the eternal flow whereby I exist at *one* with the universe. It is the seat of my divine mind, the knower, the wise woman, and the observer. It is my intuition and higher consciousness. My right mind is ever present and gets lost in time.
>
> Many of us make judgments with our left hemisphere and then are not willing to *step to the right* (that is, into the consciousness of our right hemisphere) for a file update. For many of us, once

we have made a decision, then we are attached to that
decision forever. I have found that often the last thing
a really dominating left hemisphere wants is to share
its limited cranial space with an open-minded right
counterpart![5]

What Dr. Taylor articulates so brilliantly is that it is the right
hemisphere of the brain that likely receives the intuitive knowing nonconsciously and sends it as a bolt of lightning to the left hemisphere of
the brain, where it 'zaps' into our conscious awareness. Recent research
even suggests that some intuitive information may first come through
your heart seconds before your brain registers the information. We'll
talk more about the implications of this in Chapter Six.[6]

Intellect and Intuition Collide

When your left hemisphere is 'hit' with powerful information all
at once, I believe it relaxes its judgments (releases its resistance) and
accepts the information. Or perhaps the left hemisphere releases its
resistance first in order to open up to new ways of thinking. And that
allows the answer to rush in. Think of all those times when you give up
or surrender. You let go. Moments, hours, or days later, the answer you
need rushes in. It's as if your letting go created a vacuum that allowed
the new energy of the information you needed to rush in.

The intuitive aha! wisdom collides with your intellect and then your
intellect welcomes in that wisdom. What I mean by that is you wouldn't
be able to accept the aha! if it were too far from what your existing
beliefs, attitudes, and perceptions were willing to consider. You'd find a
way to reject it. In fact, some of us who have a very vocal inner critic can
find a way to reject even a powerful aha!

A truly transformative experience—a life-changing epiphany—
occurs when, thanks to divine grace or other spiritual experience (still

involving a powerful shift in energy), you 'jump' a level or two beyond your current beliefs. Many spiritual leaders will talk of this kind of transformational experience. And, some, like the story of Saul becoming Paul in the Bible, or more recently, the transformations of spiritual leaders Eckhart Tolle and Byron Katie, seemed to involve dramatic changes in their egos or personalities in order to achieve higher or enlightened consciousness. They literally become a new person. For most of us, it's actually a lot easier, if a bit slower, to move in the same direction of higher consciousness by a series of aha! moments.

Aha! Moments as a Powerful Flow of Energy

Everything is energy, even the thoughts or inspiration that lead to aha! moments. You may have heard many times that everything is energy, but have you thought about this truth in the context of creating brilliant ideas, or gaining clarity about the right next step or decision?

When you truly internalize the knowledge that everything is energy, you begin to realize how powerful you are and why aha! moments can deliver the knowledge and clarity you need when you need it.

Thoughts are things. With today's scanning technology (functional magnetic resonance imaging, or fMRI), we can now see thoughts being formed—becoming 'things' when they 'pop' into our conscious awareness. Each thought has a vibration associated with it. The more thoughts you think at a certain vibratory level, the more you change the vibration of your body and energy field to match the vibration of those thoughts. And the more you become a beacon for whatever matches the vibration of your thoughts.

When you truly
internalize the knowledge that
everything is energy, you begin
to realize how powerful you
are and why aha! moments can
deliver the knowledge
and clarity you need when
you need it.

Dianna Amorde

We intuitively understand that aha! moments represent an influx of energy when we talk about them as a lightning bolt of information. This makes perfect sense when you realize that thoughts are bits of information that are bits of energy. When you ask for an answer to a question, you send out energy that is seeking a match (an answer). Like a radio antenna, you are both a sender of energetic information and a receiver. The information or answer that comes in does not arrive by consciously thinking of the answer or working through a decision analysis process; it simply arrives. You pick up its signal and the answer 'pops' into your head. We'll explore the possible sources of the aha! wisdom in Chapter Two.

Are You Really Stuck?

If you're creatively blocked or 'stuck' and unable to make a decision, realize that the stuck feeling makes us think that energy is not moving. However, we know that energy is always moving. The stuck feeling comes from thinking the same thoughts (at the same vibration) over and over again, so we have the *perception* that nothing is moving.

Going back to Karen's story at the beginning of the chapter, stuck meant no energy to do even the most basic things she needed to do to generate the right referrals, opportunities, and interviews. She was frozen in a loop of pros and cons about looking for a job. Imagine a ball bouncing back and forth between two options. It's stuck in a pattern and can't 'land' on an ideal option without some energy to move it in a clear direction and 'hold' it there.

Karen's aha! moment, when she saw the photo of the city of Dallas, acted as the catalyst she needed to move her toward her optimal direction, a job in Dallas. Like a rush of flowing water to break up a logjam of recurring thoughts, Karen's aha! quickly revealed the right next step and provided her with a burst of energy to follow through on the insight she received.

An Elusive Experience?

Many people assume that aha! moments are experiences of grace and divine intervention, and are therefore rare and elusive. While that may be true at times when you don't heighten your awareness and receptivity, you can actively seek out and receive aha! moments or experiences on a regular basis.

Using the idea of aha! moments as a powerful flow of energy, consider the possibility of repeatedly experiencing this flow by keeping all of your sources of energy and intelligence healthy and clear. Many of us simply need to awaken to the knowledge that mental intellect is only one—and possibly the least important—way of receiving, processing, and knowing ideas, crucial information, and ideal next steps.

Your intellect is of supreme importance when articulating a problem or creating action plans and timelines; however, its role in the creation of a new idea or solution is limited at best. Aha! moments point to the value of intuition when it comes to generating the idea or solution you need in any given moment. When you open up to the knowledge that your brain's intellectual capabilities aren't the determining factor in solving any problem and begin to turn your focus to noticing and heeding the wisdom that comes through your right brain, then you open up to regularly experiencing the power of aha! moments.

A New Approach to Decision-Making and Action

Imagine the reduction in stress, the success, and the abundance that operating from the guidance the aha's you regularly experience can bring. Why does stress go down and the possibility for success and abundance (in all forms) increase when you run your life this way? Because you are now bringing all of the resources that have always been at your disposal to every challenge you face. No longer are you relying on the thinking of your logical mind or intellect.

Living and working from the wisdom and clarity of aha! moments, with intuitive hunches or 'hits' to guide you until the next aha!, is an approach to life that makes effective use of your mental intellect without letting it be in charge. This way of running your life reminds you that you are not the thoughts you think. *You* are the soul witnessing those thoughts.

It's not always easy to approach life this way despite the enticing benefits. From the time we were small and throughout school, most of us have been programmed to rely on our intellect to guide us and have been told repeatedly that logical thinking and deductive reasoning are superior to any other ways of knowing. We've also been counseled to seek expert opinions and facts and to rely on those when we're not sure what the next step should be.

There was an article in *Newsweek* in 2008 about a psychic to whom businessmen and -women were paying large sums of money to help them make the right decisions regarding investments and other business opportunities.[7] I'm very open to psychics and have enjoyed some powerful readings. They can serve to help you see the world differently, open you up to new possibilities, and give you the courage to take a step you've wanted to take all along.

But here's the funny thing about hiring a psychic to help you make a decision. You still have to make the call. Only this time, the decision is about whether you buy into the insight or 'gut' of the psychic. The woman interviewed admitted that she wasn't always accurate, but clearly she was accurate enough to gain a large following and make hundreds of thousands of dollars. Even so, if you hired her, you'd still have to make the final decision.

How will you make the big and small decisions in your life? My objective with this book is to help you realize that you're already receiving all of the indicators you need to make the optimal decision, with or without extensive research or a psychic's input. All you need is to start paying close attention to the most fascinating person in your world: you!

See yourself as the expert to rely on when it comes time to make an important decision (or even a not-so-important decision). As the key player in the scene that unfolds *after* any decision you make, it's vital that you clearly understand how you perceive the situation and how you feel about your decision.

Embrace Your Unique Perspective

Research tells us that no two brains are wired the same way.[8] We are all unique in how we perceive the world and react to what happens around and to us. Our interpretations of what happens around and to us are based upon all of our experiences from the moment we are born (if not before). Every new piece of information you receive and the accompanying emotional interpretation of that information or experience affects the wiring of your brain.

In addition, we now know that the non- or 'sub' conscious segment of our brain assumes the pictures we create in our heads of what happened in the past, what we want to happen, and what might happen (whether consciously created or not) are real. Our pictures or visualizations are sometimes based upon what we *consciously* choose to create or imagine, but, more likely, they're based upon stored memories, beliefs, and attitudes associated with past experiences, even scenes from movies we've watched.

You have a vast array of hidden beliefs based upon all of the experiences of your life, especially those thoughts or beliefs imparted to you by your parents, your teachers, and others when you were a child.

Taken all together, this means that no research, no matter how thorough, can accurately determine what the right decision is for you: whether it's a decision to proceed with surgery, take an experimental drug, buy a business, hire a new employee, or take skydiving lessons. This is why I believe it's so critical that we each regain our ability to recognize, respect, access, and effectively use our intuitive abilities and to cultivate those aha! moments that bring such clarity.

It can be challenging to assess whether an intuitive 'hit' was really accurate guidance; a mistaken 'leap' made by the brain's powerful, but not 100 percent accurate, ability to recognize patterns; or wishful or fearful thinking. But an aha! moment is so strong and clear that we can confidently use it to guide us forward. We'll talk about why that's true in the next chapter.

It is possible to live your life by seeking out and trusting aha! moments, trusting your innate wisdom. This book will teach you how to do this. I stumble and fumble my way through some days, but I can honestly say that when I give myself permission to run my days predominantly through aha's! and hunches, my days flow with joy, grace, and ease. When I don't, I struggle.

As the world continues to speed up around us, with faster and faster changes in technology, consumer products, and even our physical surroundings, we can easily get overwhelmed and find it difficult to make the necessary decisions to move our life and career in the direction we want it to go. Focusing on effectively using our aha! moments and intuitive hunches enables us to slow the world down and operate from our full brilliance.

The most effective decisions are made when you access all of the information available to you, including your aha! moments. So let's begin to harness your ability to brilliantly guide your work and life in its ideal direction. It's time to wake up to your potential to live life from one aha! moment to another.

Inspired Questions, Actions, and Leaps

✳ Have you or any of your friends or family ever experienced any aha! moments? Any hunches? Any gut feelings? Did you heed them? What happened?

✳ Think back to any aha! moments or hunches you've experienced. How did you *know* it was an aha! moment or a hunch?

✳ What makes an insight or aha! true or real for you? Is it a certain feeling or experience in your body?

✳ Write down any 'clues' that tell you that you've experienced an aha! moment. If you haven't experienced any, ask your friends or family to describe their aha! moments. Are there any commonalities between them?

✳ When are you willing to take a *leap* toward something? It's a leap in a new direction or toward something because there's a chasm between what you know (facts, data, expert advice) and what you feel inspired to go for. What was the last leap you took?

Need an Aha! Moment? Try This:

Write a letter to your nonconscious mind or Higher Self.[9] This activity is especially effective when you write your letter just before you go to bed, as it gives your nonconscious something to work on while you're sleeping. The key elements of your letter need to be:

1. Write the problem, challenge, or question you need help with as clearly as possible. If you can't articulate your question, it will be difficult for your nonconscious mind to find the answer.

2. Ask for the answer within 24 or 48 hours. Keep the deadline tight enough, so you'll remember to 'look' for the answer.

3. Ask for the answer to be as clear as possible (easy for you to understand).

4. Write "thank you for your help."

5. Sign your name.

6. Place your letter in an envelope and place it somewhere you'll see it and be reminded to look for the answer. Finally, be open to your answer coming via an intuitive hunch to flip through a magazine, talk to someone new, or turn on the radio. Images, lyrics of songs, books, and people stopping to talk with you, can all be ways your Higher Self or nonconsicous mind will guide you to the answer.

7. If the answer still hasn't come after 24 to 48 hours, write a note on your letter reminding your nonconscious to deliver the answer you need now.

Chapter Two **Your Energetic System of Knowing**

Gordon's passion is constructing new buildings or structures. He would describe himself as simply a builder. However, Gordon has a bit of a challenge. He doesn't like math and has never been very good at it. You might think that's no problem for a builder, but consider the challenge of the planned slope or angle of a roof. Normally, you'd need to measure and calculate what will and won't work. Unfortunately, that's not something Gordon is comfortable doing. But Gordon has another way of solving these kinds of problems. It's worked for him in the past and it worked for him this time.

Gordon dreamt the answer to his question—his aha! moment. At night, before going to bed, Gordon got clear in his mind the challenge of how to redesign the roof for the current project he was working on. While he slept, his nonconscious mind worked on the problem. When Gordon woke up, he had a clear image of the new, revised roof that he had 'dreamt' while he slept. He jumped out of bed, ready to try this new image out, and was thrilled that his source of aha! moments had worked again.

When Gordon went to work that morning, he drew the image that he saw in his mind and shared it with his team. It was a perfect solution and his co-workers told him so. When asked how he figured it out, he said, "I dreamed it." "Ha-ha," they said. "No, really," said Gordon. "I dreamt the solution."

Where Do Aha! Moments Come From?

One of the biggest reasons many of us don't follow through on our intuitive hunches, or even our powerful aha! moments, is that we don't know how we know what we know. Our inner critic, outside experts, coworkers, bosses, and family members can derail our best intentions to follow through on what we've come to know inside. Research supports this regular occurrence, as your rational left brain tends to dominate the intuitive right brain.[10]

One of the best ways to silence, or at least tone down, the opinions of the inner critic (and others), is to beat it at its own game. By understanding how the brain works and where at least some of our knowing comes from, we can boost our own confidence in heeding the wisdom of aha! moments and pursuing our intuitive hunches.

How does the brain receive and acknowledge aha! moments? Where did Gordon's answer—the image of the correct, new slope for his building—come from? Where do all of our aha! moments come from? The answers to these questions are still unfolding, as the work of neuroscientists, quantum physicists, biologists, cardiologists, and others reveal different pieces of the puzzle. And, obviously, as new information in one area comes to light, it affects how we view and understand information in other areas.

Generally speaking, aha! moments come from all of the sources of information we have access to. Most of us think about tangible sources of information: data, facts, history, expert opinion, and memories that our brain has access to. While those typical sources are the easiest for most of us to wrap our minds around and to prove, when you step back and broaden your perspective, it's highly likely that we have other, less tangible sources of information or knowing.

In Gordon's case, his answer probably came via stored knowledge in his brain or body. Being a builder, he obviously has a wealth of experience, training, and education in the form of stored memories to call on to answer his question. Someone with no issues with math might effortlessly draw on all of this knowledge to consciously calculate the ideal solution. However, Gordon needed to obtain the answer a different way. His right brain likely compensated for his inability to do the math by creating a picture from his knowledge and delivering it to him via a dream.

One Source of Knowing: Your Stored Experiences

Your brain is estimated to be roughly one-sixths conscious and five-sixths nonconscious.[11] This one-sixth is the part of your brain that sleeps when you do. It's also the part of the brain that's associated with consciously *thinking* about and solving a challenge.

Research shows that the nonconscious part of your brain is still active and working or processing while you sleep. That's likely why asking your nonconscious mind to work on a challenge just before you go to sleep, like Gordon did, can help you receive the answer or idea you need immediately upon waking, or soon after. From experience, Gordon knew that his brain could solve the problem for him while he slept. So he deliberately posed a question that could generate the image of the new roof of his building. Consciously doing this on a regular basis can be a powerful way to solve problems or at least send you down the right path for the solution.

When this hard-working, but consciously inaccessible part of your brain—your nonconscious mind—'sends' an answer into your conscious awareness, it seems to you as if it just 'popped' into your head. And in some cases, the answer comes so quickly, it's hard to imagine that it's not a brand-new thought divinely sent or—as your inner critic would tell you—foolishly guessed. However, remember just how much knowledge your nonconscious mind has access to before dismissing your intuitive hunch as ridiculous or less worthy of consideration than the data laid out before you.

Why should you pay any attention to a thought or idea that 'pops' into your head? Because beneath your conscious awareness, your brain is rapidly searching its databank of stored information to see if it has the answer you need. This databank is filled with all of the memories experienced in your lifetime. This is why intuitive wisdom increases with age and experience on a job. Your expertise is greater than you think.

Your databank of stored information is more likely to include memories with some emotion attached to them.[12] The more intense the emotion associated with the memory, the easier it is to bring up in some detail. These memories are not necessarily memories that can be recalled in enough detail to verbalize, but they may evoke an image or an emotion.

There are arguments about where memories are stored. Some scientists believe they are located throughout the brain. Others point to research that shows how different areas of the body store memories, especially traumatic memories. Anyone who's ever experienced an emotional release during a massage or chiropractic treatment can vouch for the truth of body memory. Even more fascinating is the theory that memories, as bits of energy, are stored in our energy field and retrieved as needed by the brain. Wherever this information may be stored, your brain relies heavily on it to quickly come up with an answer. Actively thinking takes considerable energy, so your brain would much prefer to pull an answer out of its 'warehouse' than to think up a new solution.

Pattern Recognition—A Sometimes Faulty System for Delivering Quick Solutions

Your brain likely developed its ability of pattern recognition or memory match to conserve energy because it does not create or store energy. It's an energy hog. Your brain uses up to 20 percent or more of your body's store of energy at any given time while weighing only a measly three pounds, less than three percent of your body weight. This fact really hit home for me while reading Danah Zohar's fascinating book, *Rewiring the Corporate Brain*:

> A learning, creative brain uses more energy than the whole rest of the body put together. Out of the box, at-the-edge thinking uses as much energy as a game of rugby football. If we were creative all of the time, we would get exhausted.[13]

Having watched a rugby game, Zohar's example painted a compelling picture of how hard my brain works when it's creating something new and helped me understand the gift of pattern recognition. Our brain's ability to recognize a situation it has seen before enables it to take an energy-saving shortcut and jump to an answer.

When you are 'searching' for an answer to a question or for a possible solution to a problem, you are burning up precious energy. Therefore, your nonconscious mind rapidly searches through its vast storehouse of experience to see if there is a pattern or vibrational match for what you've requested. If it finds a match, it will quickly send the information up to your conscious mind.

However, your brain's desire to take shortcuts and use pattern recognition whenever possible is also the reason why many people say that intuition can be wrong. Sometimes your brain will jump to a conclusion only for you to later realize that a few key pieces of information were missing and therefore it was wrong. Or your brain will incorrectly link a hidden childhood memory with a present situation and, for example, tell you not to hire or work with someone.

For example, imagine that you're trying to hire the ideal candidate for a new job. You can't help but have a gut reaction to every candidate you meet. You'll think it's your intuition or inner knowing working again to steer you from someone you've decided is an undesirable candidate when, in fact, your intuition came from a mistaken visual 'match' between the candidate and a relative you can't stand. Your brain did its job of protecting you, but the poor, unsuspecting job applicant—who's a dead ringer for your Uncle Norris—can't figure out why he wasn't hired.

Pause Before You Leap

In his thought-provoking book, *On Being Certain*, neuroscientist Robert Burton, M.D., points out that all thoughts 'percolate up from the unconscious' (or, as I describe it, the nonconscious). So, just because a thought 'pops into our head' from our nonconscious mind does not make it accurate intuitive information or a powerful aha! moment. As Dr. Burton suggests, "The issue isn't whether or not unconscious thoughts can be of great value, but in sorting out those that are from those that aren't."[14]

Not all 'feelings of knowing,' as Dr. Burton describes the sense of correctness we feel when we have thoughts or ideas resonate with us, whether from intuition or conscious thinking, are accurate. Our brain can and does trick us from time to time, so we need to be careful about knee-jerk responses to our intuitive hunches. Chapter Three addresses the need for a 'wise mind' approach to decision-making and Chapter Eight provides detailed steps to help you confidently trust your intuitive insights.

Despite the drawbacks of our brain's talent for pattern recognition and the more subtle intuitive hunches or ideas that pop into our heads, our ability to rapidly pull up stored data, even old beliefs and memories, is a true gift that we need to honor. Even in the case of the job applicant example, you still made the correct decision for you at that moment in time. If hired despite your gut rejection of him, that poor soul would never have had a chance to succeed. Only if you were able to bring to conscious awareness the connection between him and Uncle Norris would you have been able to break away from your intense dislike of the new employee. It can be challenging for any of us, even people who are highly attuned to their intuition and who know themselves well, to know when we're truly receiving intuitive information and when we're allowing past fears, biases, or wishful thinking to influence us. That's why aha! moments are so valuable and worth actively seeking out.

The Power of Aha! Moments

Aha! moments rarely rely on pattern recognition. From my experience, true intuition is like an aha! moment because the answer resonates within you in multiple ways. If you only had the quick answer that popped into your head to guide you, you would be right to be cautious and explore a little further. However, if you had a strong emotional signal, a clear physical signal, and a compelling spiritual connection, then you'd have an aha! moment and could trust the 'truth' of the statement, idea, or experience for you.

The Energetic System of Knowing™

Consider the possibility that the idea or answer you need comes into your awareness via what I call an Energetic System of Knowing, which consists of four channels of energy or knowing: mental, emotional, physical, and spiritual.

While I will discuss each of these channels of energy or knowing in detail later, all four channels of knowing appear to have access, to varying degrees, to a wide body of knowledge that you are rarely conscious of. The reason an aha! experience is so memorable or powerful is because of the flow of energy—the bigger the aha!, the more intense the flow of energy. "It felt like I was hit by a lightning bolt," many of us say after an aha! moment. That figure of speech is reflecting an intuitive sense of what went on within you.

At the time you realize the aha!, you simultaneously receive signals of information from all four ways of knowing:

Mental — Intellect (Left Brain) Collides with:

Emotional — Intuitive (Right Brain)

Physical — Intuitive (Right Brain)

Spiritual — Intuitive (Right Brain)

✳ **Mental.** The answer, idea, or insight incorporates all of your intelligence, learning, beliefs, and assumptions to date. It doesn't stretch too far beyond your current perceptions. For example, if you grew up in a small town in Idaho and currently live in Boise, the state capital, you likely have some set beliefs about where you'd be comfortable and willing to live. Now imagine you've gone to hear an expert in your industry talk about the ultimate keys to success. He tells the audience that the latest trends in the industry suggest a move to Lima,

Peru is the key to your success. In fact, he's so sure this will be the hub of your industry, he's moving there himself in 60 days! It's highly unlikely that you'd even be able to consider that possibility or acknowledge it, let alone have it register as an aha! moment. It's too far out of your comfort zone and beliefs about how you plan to live your life. Your left brain, which doesn't like change, would reject it immediately.

While most of us tend to focus exclusively on developing and using this form of intelligence or knowing, it is only *one* of the ways of receiving and processing information and is the strength of the left hemisphere of your brain. Despite its elevation to god-like status among many intellectuals, your Mental or Intellectual Knowing alone will *never* lead you to an aha! moment.

✳ **Emotional.** There is a powerful feeling of rightness, joy, and peace (not to mention relief, if you've been trying to gain clarity for a while) that accompanies the insight. You *feel* the 'fit' of the solution for you. Your emotions (energy in motion) are arguably the best indicator of when you're moving in a direction (thoughts and action) that serves you or in a direction that's unhealthy or away from your values. That emotional connection comes through via your intuition and the right hemisphere of your brain.

✳ **Physical.** There is a physical manifestation that signals the truth or accuracy of the idea to you. This is usually a feeling of warmth in the gut, a warm glow in the heart, goosebumps, chills up and down the spine, or other physical experiences that are unique, but meaningful, to you. It's been said that your body never lies. Consider the possibility that your body not only never lies, but it senses what's best for you as well. Your body reveals valuable information to you if you will only pay attention. You'll need your intuition and the right hemisphere of your brain to unlock its wisdom.

✳ **Spiritual.** The answer, idea, or insight aligns perfectly with your highest values and your Highest Self or soul. You have a sense that the wisdom is divinely given, even if you don't consider yourself a particularly spiritual person. Considered the most powerful energy force on the planet by many, even though it's not yet quantifiable; this is the energy that sustains someone when they're fighting for what they believe in despite lack of sleep and resources, running the twenty-fifth mile of the marathon, lifting a car to save their child, or performing any other feat that appears mentally and physically impossible.

Because the signal or information reaches you simultaneously with the aha! moment's taking place, you can literally feel a jolt of recognition, confidence, or clarity that causes you to (at least internally) go aha! Your aha! might also come via a powerful dream and upon waking you realize the dream was an aha! experience. You receive the same clarity in all four ways of knowing. Whether it's an immediate aha! or a delayed aha! moment brought on by a dream, you ultimately experience the same sense of peace that comes from finally receiving the clarity you need.

Sources of Knowing: The Past and Present Thoughts of Others

You are far more brilliant than you *think* you are, simply because your brain has access to all of your rich life experiences, whether you can consciously remember them or not. While some experts believe those experiences and the beliefs that arise from them are the only source of intuitive information, I believe that's really only a small part of the knowledge you have access to.

You may also have the ability to tap into the wisdom of those who came before you and those who are on this planet now (and, who knows, maybe even the wisdom of the future). How is that possible? Remember that thoughts are energetic 'things' that do not die when the physical person is no longer here. Regardless of whether you believe in reincarnation or that our spirits live on after our physical death, we know that each thought we think has a vibration or life of its own.

Once you consciously think a thought, it becomes a vibrational reality that can be viewed with scanning technology (functional magnetic resonance imaging [fMRI]). In *The Intention Experiment*, author and award-winning journalist Lynne McTaggart—an expert on bringing leading-edge science to the rest of us—shares some of the exciting research that points to the profound intelligence of this universe and the leading role we play in it. From our thoughts to our emotions to our intentions and perceptions, we appear to create the world we expect to see and communicate (transfer energy) much more than we ever imagined.

> A sizable body of research exploring the nature of consciousness, carried on for more than thirty years in prestigious scientific institutions around the world, shows that thoughts are capable of affecting everything from the simplest machines to the most complex living beings. This evidence suggests that human thoughts and intentions are an actual physical 'something' with the astonishing power to change our world.[15]
>
> —*Lynne McTaggart*

This evidence suggests that human thoughts and intentions are an actual physical 'something' with the astonishing power to change our world.

Lynne McTaggart

We generate thousands of random thoughts a day that don't do very much. These aren't the thoughts that have a lot of power (at least not until they coalesce into a belief or strong vibration). According to scientist Valerie Hunt, Ph.D., author of *Infinite Mind* and former UCLA professor, most of our random thoughts stay within our own energy field. We have little power to propel them out into the universe and possibly another's energy field. However, those thoughts that have a strong emotion associated with them or clear intent are likely to be broadcast out into the universe and 'picked up' or 'read' by others who are receptive or open to the vibration associated with your thought.[16]

Study after study supports the ability to 'read' minds or pick up on thoughts thousands of miles away. Many of us still don't trust this idea. Perhaps that's because most of us can't begin to replicate the idea of reading someone's mind. That said, I bet you can remember times when a spouse or dear friend seemed to read your mind or finish your sentences. Perhaps this experience resulted from co-mingling your energy fields.

Consider the possibility that you (your logical, analytical mind) are likely blocking the reception of any thoughts or intuitions from others because of fears about the changes the information may bring, the responsibility associated with receiving so much information, or the fear that the information is inauthentic or from a negative presence (depending upon what your spiritual beliefs are).

How Much Information Do You Want Access To?

In a guided meditation offered in my intuition workshops participants are asked to choose which of five hypothetical doors they want to visualize opening. Each door represents how much knowledge each individual is willing to have access to. Depending upon your curiosity and openness to new sources of information, you might choose the 'door' that represents accessing only stored memories within your brain and body, or you might choose door number five which represents access to all that is, all that ever was, and all that will be.

Remember the truth that all pieces of information are bits of energy, and each of us is like a radio antenna, sending and receiving bits of energy or information out into the universe. So, each hypothetical door also represents how strong of a signal you're willing to send and receive. When you start to open up to the idea you've got a lot more control over what kind of information you receive and what you do with that information, then you can begin to consciously relax and take steps to increase your access to and conscious awareness of the vast knowledge that science is beginning to discover is within our reach at any given moment.

With practice, you can 'pick up' powerful thoughts (with emotion and/or strong intent associated with them) from people around the world if you choose to. This isn't about literally reading word-for-word your friend's or spouse's every thought; it's about being sensitive to the energy of the thoughts around you, so you can better communicate, change your negotiation tactics in a critical business discussion, make better decisions in all areas of your life, and be better informed.

What Makes an Aha! Moment Unique

What makes an aha! moment different from an intuitive hunch or 'hit' is not the source of information—both aha's and intuitive 'hits' can include the same sources—it's the number of sources of information involved, the energetic strength of the information coming in, the amount of resistance the piece of information has to overcome, and how important it is to you at the time. This is why the title of this book includes the phrase 'when intellect and intuition collide.'

Within you, your intellect (Mental Energy) finally relaxes and opens up to other possibilities. It enables a force of energy from your intuitive ways of knowing (Emotional, Physical, and Spiritual) to 'collide' with it to create the aha! moment.

Why are there three forms of intuitive knowing and only one form of intellectual knowing? I believe it relates to the way your brain and body are wired. Just as the vast majority of your brain power is nonconscious and accessed intuitively, you receive the vast majority of your information intuitively. This makes perfect sense because it minimizes what comes into your conscious awareness. Remember that your brain can't store energy and uses a lot of it to think through problems.

Intuitive knowing, which comes to you or pops into your head, takes a lot less effort to work with than trying to mentally work through an answer. For example, trusting your hunch that the information you're looking for is in the addendum or on page 156 of that research report is a heck of a lot less taxing than insisting on skimming each page to find that all-important quote for your presentation.

When you consider that everything is energy and is communicating on some level all of the time, it's wise to have your body, emotions, soul, and nonconscious mind handle most of that information. Think of the overload to your mind if every bit of sensory information came into your conscious awareness! The challenge comes from your logical, thinking mind placing great emphasis on what it can sense—and thus consciously think about—with your five senses. It doesn't know how to process information that comes from your heart (emotions), soul, and the energy all around you, so it dismisses it. And so do most people.

Like the clients who experience my guided visualizations, you can begin to imagine that you are a unique, powerful field of energy that transmits and receives information throughout the universe. You truly are able to access all that is, all that was, and all that ever will be via your Energetic System of Knowing. But because of your unique filter—all the experiences that have shaped you—what you receive is unique to you.

When you deny the reality that you are an energetic being capable of receiving information or intelligence—bits of energy—from many sources, you deny your power. Quantum physics tells us that time is our creation, as is the sense that we are solid bodies, sitting in solid chairs. The reality is that we live in a fluid world with at least all past and present thoughts available at any given moment. Perhaps we can even tap into future thinking or possible outcomes.

What makes all of this critically important is that your brain is unique. It filters information that it receives differently than anyone else's brain. So, if one hundred people tap into exactly the same intelligence or knowing to come up with the solution to global warming, none of them will process that intelligence the same way you do. Just as a corporate brainstorming session is diminished when all attendees fail to speak up or participate, if you fail to use all of the wisdom to which you have access both you and the world will be diminished or at least less than what you could be.

I'm reminded of the famous quote from the late Martha Graham, a truly inspired dancer and leader. Graham was talking with Agnes de Mille, another revered dancer, when she offered de Mille these stirring words of encouragement:

> There is a vitality, a life force, a quickening that is translated through you into action, and there is only one of you in all time, this expression is unique, and if you block it, it will never exist through any other medium; and be lost. The world will not have it. It is not your business to determine how good it is, nor how valuable, nor how it compares with other expression. It is your business to keep it yours clearly and directly, to *keep the channel open*.[17] [emphasis added]

*There is a vitality,
a life force, a quickening that
is translated through you into
action, and there is only one of
you in all time, this expression
is unique, and if you block it,
it will never exist through any
other medium; and be lost.*

Martha Graham

What if Martha Graham was right? Only this 'vitality and life force' is not just about the inspired movement of a dancer or other artist, but also about the creativity, inspiration, direction, and decisions that guide *your* work and life. If you do not open up to all your channels of knowing, you deny yourself and others the creative brilliance that only you can bring to any challenge, creative endeavor, or decision you are a part of.

Inspired Questions, Actions, and Leaps

✻ Think about the last aha! you experienced. Do you have any recollection of the associated emotions or feelings in your body that accompanied the aha! experience?

✻ Looking back, can you envision how the information came to you as a 'bolt' of energy in your body, mind, and soul?

✻ Now think about your decision-making process. Do you try to rely solely on historical data or expert opinion, or do you check in with your gut or intuition? Do you pay attention to your feelings? Do you consciously check to see if your decision fits with your values or soul?

✻ If you check in with your intuition, how do you know you've experienced intuitive information? Any signs in your body? Any emotions?

✻ Do you sleep on your decision, or let it 'sit' with you before moving forward? How do you later know the answer is right for you?

✻ The next time you need to make a decision, try consciously checking in with these different channels of knowing. See whether that makes you feel more confident about your decision. We'll discuss a specific process for doing this in Chapter Eight.

✳ How have you experienced and used the 'vitality and life force' Martha Graham spoke of? How can you consciously incorporate her wisdom into your daily work?

. . . .
The Sound of Clarity

✳ Try making the separate sounds of 'ah' and 'ha.' Ah is a sound of release and relaxation—you drop your resistance to allow the wisdom you need to flow in. Ha is the sound of joy and laughter at having found the idea or solution you need.

✳ You can increase the likelihood of receiving aha! moments by practicing speaking these sounds aloud. Feel the difference in your energy after a few moments of experiencing the sounds of clarity. Try saying ah ten times (breathe in deeply and exhale the ah) and do the same with ha after you're done. Now that you've got a goofy smile on your face and you're literally 'humming,' read on.

. . . .
Need an Aha! Moment? Try This:

Ask Questions. If you want to know why you feel the way you do about a decision, ask yourself open-ended questions and sit quietly to see what pops into your head. If sitting quietly doesn't work, ask your questions just before you go to bed, when you wake up (have a note by your bedside to remind you), or when you step into the shower.

By consciously asking yourself questions and waiting for an answer, you're sending a message to your nonconscious mind or Higher Self that you really want to know the answer. The key is to actually wait a few moments or overnight for the answer before distracting yourself with thoughts about all you have to do, what went wrong during the day, and so on.

Aha!

Chapter Three **Use Your Wise Mind**

Kevin had been out of the entertainment industry for a few years, pursuing other opportunities. As Kevin became more and more disenchanted with what he was doing, his confidence in his abilities naturally began to waver. So, when the idea to go back to the industry he loved— wiser and with clarity about what he wanted—popped into his head, Kevin did what most of us would do. He began to 'think' about his idea, which included discussing it with trusted friends and peers to see what they thought.

Unfortunately, Kevin's intuitive hunch to go back to an industry he loved wasn't initially strong enough to be a truly aha! moment. So he quickly veered into his left brain to think through his idea. This created a big problem for him for a few reasons: 1. Kevin was feeling a bit down about himself and therefore very vulnerable to his inner critic (who will say anything to get us to avoid making a change) and 2. being vulnerable made Kevin susceptible to well-meaning, but ultimately irrelevant, data offered by his friends.

When his friends offered up the 'wisdom' that two years is too much time out of the entertainment industry, and 'history' shows that being away from the marketplace that long will make it too difficult for you to get back in, Kevin's inner critic reinforced this message with reminders of all of his past mistakes. So Kevin began to seriously consider that maybe he wasn't that good at what he did, maybe he had been out of the industry too long, and maybe he wouldn't be able to convince anyone to take a chance on him.

His mind quickly created all kinds of negative results from all of these maybe's. The idea flashed into his consciousness that he'd be forced to take a lower-level job, which would look terrible on his resume, set him back for life, and so on. "So why had I even considered this stupid idea?" he thought to himself.

After leaving him a voicemail that gently (at least in my mind), but compellingly, kicked him in the butt and reminded him of how talented and powerful he was, he called me back a day later and said, "Dianna, you heal people! Thank you!" Kevin's imagination (right brain) was ignited by what I said and he regained a more balanced view of himself. He became re-energized and focused on finding the right next job in the industry he loved.

I'm sure you've had something like Kevin's internal dialogue with yourself a time or two. When this happens, we can easily slide into despair or stay 'stuck' in this thought loop, remaining in a job or an industry we dislike because we feel there is no other option. We're caught up in our heads—our own thoughts and the thoughts and 'facts' (our rational mind loves those) offered up to us by experts and friends.

Kevin finally realized that he was a unique individual and no historical data could possibly represent who he was, what he brought to a job, and what the situation was in the present moment. When you allow all of your inner wisdom to blend with 'the facts,' you move into your 'wise mind' and can now make the optimal decision for yourself.

Work From Your Wise Mind

The ability to optimally draw upon the talents of both hemispheres of the brain is referred to as having a 'wise mind.' My understanding is that the concept of wise mind was first developed in association with Dialectical Behavioral Therapy (DBT). DBT patients who suffer from severe depression or suicidal thoughts are taught to blend their rational or reasonable mind (left brain) and their emotional or intuitive mind (right brain) in order to move out of the over-active right brain (flooded with emotions) to think clearly.

In her excellent book, *Awakening Intuition*, Mona Lisa Schulz, M.D., Ph.D.—a neuropsychiatrist, neuroscientist, and medical intuitive—points out that wise mind is actually a great reminder of why we need a *balanced* blend of *both* the rational mind and the intuitive, emotional mind.

> This balance is demonstrably beneficial. It's been shown that true geniuses have a more fluid partnership between the two hemispheres than most people, a greater ability to switch rapidly and smoothly between the two. They demonstrate flexibility, as opposed to the rigid hemispheric reaction most people exhibit to a problem.[18]

The Wise Mind

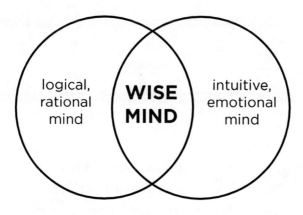

logical, rational mind   **WISE MIND**   intuitive, emotional mind

An aha! moment allows you to fully experience the wisdom and clarity that comes from actively engaging both sides of your brain— using your wise mind. As Dr. Schulz notes, research supports that genius is the ability to *effectively* use both hemispheres of the brain. Again, as noted in Chapter One, we use both hemispheres all of the time, but we don't always use them optimally.

Dr. Schulz, as a unique combination of neuropsychiatrist, neuroscientist, and medical intuitive, is a great example of someone who experiences much of her work and life in her wise mind. Most of us are not there yet, and, unlike the patients who need to move *left* toward their rational mind in order to reach wise mind, many of us need to move *right* toward our intuitive, emotional mind.

Peter Senge, author of the classic management book, *The Fifth Discipline*, notes that we're mistaken if we see rational thinking and intuition as opposites and that the integration of reason and intuition is a sign of personal mastery.[19] Our objective isn't to choose one type of thinking or processing over another, it's to embrace and integrate both, knowing when to emphasize our intuitive channels of knowing and when to rely on our mental channel of knowing.

Wise Mind: Where Aha! Moments Reside

Importantly, as one student of Dialectical Behavioral Therapy (DBT) indicates below, the wise mind is also the way we access aha! moments or experiences and then process or take action on them. It is the state of mind that allows both intellectual and intuitive information to be honored and paid attention to.

> The funny thing about wise mind is that, most often, it finds me, more than I find it. I mean, it's clear that I've had a 'wise mind moment' when that 'aha' happens, or when I'm reflecting on something and

suddenly it all seems clear and I'm in the big picture
and feel confident about what's going on. Those are like
wonderful moments of inspiration. But I haven't yet
been able to consciously cultivate this sensation.[20]

The woman who shared these thoughts articulates beautifully what happens when we move into our wise mind and while neither she nor you might be able to consciously cultivate this experience now, that's what this book will teach you to do.

Because most of us have spent the majority of our lives trained to believe in the superiority of the rational mind and thus educated to rely on it, this book is focused on helping you regain the strength you need in your intuitive mind. When you give yourself permission to 'step to the right,' you open up to a tremendous opportunity for living a life full of aha! moments. And, even if you consider yourself intuitive or a right-brained person, it's highly likely that you could use some additional support in generating aha! moments and knowing how to use them to make better decisions.

By blending the strengths of both the left and right hemispheres of your brain—developing your wise mind—you are able to tap into and experience the clarity and peace that comes with an aha! moment.

Let Your Left Brain Relax and Receive

When you experience an aha! moment, the energies from all of your sources of knowing (mental, emotional, physical, and spiritual) are in harmony and flowing in the same direction. While normally your intellect will challenge and attempt to lead or even override the intuitive side, an aha! moment occurs when you relax your resistance and allow the intuitive information from the three other sources of knowing to rush into your awareness. You've likely experienced the power of relaxing your left brain, even if you didn't think of it that way. Have you ever walked away from a problem, gone for a run, done the dishes, or taken a shower, only to have the answer you've struggled over finally pop into your head? That's an example of the power of relaxing or disengaging to allow the aha! moment to happen.

Now imagine the left brain is 'thinking,' *pushing* energy, thought, or information in one direction ("I know this is the right approach to solving this problem," your left brain says. And then it proceeds to ignore any other information that comes in). The right brain is over on the right, doing its thing, receiving all sorts of information from a wide variety of sources. The ideas, guidance, and answers are piling up, but you aren't aware of them. Maybe they're sitting just outside your energy or auric field. Maybe they've made it to your nonconscious mind. It doesn't matter. You're so busy thinking and doing, you can't register the information.

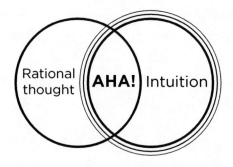

In order for an aha! moment to occur, the left brain has to relax, stop pushing, and drift (or leap?) to the right. As Jill Bolte Taylor notes, "our western society honors and rewards the skills of our 'doing' left brain," so you'll need to relax or unlearn some of those skills. Figuratively, when those circles overlap, 'bam!' Although, it's really less of a collision between intellect and intuition then it is a releasing of resistance by you.

Our western society honors and rewards the skills of our 'doing' left brain much more than our 'being' right brain. Thus, if you are having difficulty accessing the consciousness of your right mind circuitry, then it is probably because you have done a stupendous job learning exactly what you were taught while growing up. [21]

Jill Bolte Taylor, Ph.D.

Keep the Channels Open

To operate from your wise mind is to embrace and be open to all four channels of your Energetic System of Knowing. We're out of our wise mind when one channel is so wide open it floods the system and obscures the knowledge of the other three or when we elevate one channel to the exclusion of the others.

Like Dr. Schulz, psychiatrist Judith Orloff, M.D., believes in using intuition, as well as energy management, as part of any healing process. The author of numerous books, including *Positive Energy*, and assistant clinical professor of psychiatry at UCLA, Dr. Orloff describes herself as an *intuitive empath*.[22] An empath or intuitive empath is extremely sensitive to the energy, especially emotions, around them. They have a wide-open emotional channel of knowing and need to take steps to minimize its influence; otherwise, they're easily overwhelmed.

While a certain amount of empathy is highly desirable, especially in professions like nursing, being so sensitive to the emotions of people around you can obviously be a challenge. However, when their wide-open emotional channel is acknowledged and managed properly, empaths can be like Dr. Orloff and use that sensitivity to bring a unique level of insight and intelligence to their work.

How Sensitive Are Your Energetic Channels?

Perhaps, like Dr. Orloff, you have a heightened sensitivity to the emotional energy around you and are easily affected by strong emotions emanating from people, particularly in a group setting. Or, you might be fine when it comes to sensing emotions, but have an overly stimulated or open mental channel. Are you prone to putting yourself in an endless loop of thinking, obsessed with finding all possible sources of data to incorporate in any decision you need to make, intent on using only proven, thoroughly researched data, and so on? If so, you might need to turn off intellectual stimulation for awhile and focus on the other three areas of knowing.

In the physical channel, you can easily turn into a hypochondriac, only in this case, you'd be obsessed with finding the hidden meaning behind every ache, pain, and shift in your body. And, finally, an overly stimulated spiritual channel would be like walking around with your head in the clouds, unable to function in the world because you're so busy talking to God or connecting to Source, however you define it.

It is the healthy blend of all four channels of knowing that enables you to operate from your wise mind and to experience all of the aha! moments you need. You are a genius. Or you have the potential to be a genius. But it can't happen unless you access all of the knowledge at your disposal and process that knowledge from your wise mind.

Maybe you're meant to be a genius at mowing lawns. Maybe you're meant to be a genius at creating alternative fuel or addressing the challenges of global warming. You're the only one who knows what your genius is. And my guess is that you're barely tapping the surface of your potential. Like a clogged artery that inhibits the flow of blood and drains you of your energy, when you refuse to acknowledge and receive the wisdom of all four of your channels of knowing, you severely weaken your intelligence—your genius. Isn't it time to step into your wise mind and find out what you're truly capable of?

....

Inspired Questions, Actions, and Leaps

✳ Have you ever been so caught up in the data that you couldn't make a decision? How would you use the concept of wise mind to ensure you never got stuck in that situation again?

✳ Have you ever been so flooded with emotion that you made a poor decision or couldn't make a decision? Go back to one of those decisions and imagine a different outcome by talking yourself into your wise mind. How would you do it? (To find out more about the process psychiatrists use, go to www.dbtselfhelp.com or contact a mental health professional).

✳ Take a moment to consider what your 'genius' is. Don't worry about whether it has anything to do with your current job. What are you a master at and could be even better at if you always operated from your wise mind, and with all four channels open?

✳ How can you apply your understanding of what your genius is to the work you do and the life you live? Are you making the most of this unique ability?

....

Need An Aha! Moment? Try This!

Affirm the Power of Your Intuition. To better access the right hemisphere of your wise mind, reinforce the strength of your intuitive abilities. Remember, our nonconscious mind takes what we tell it and the images we give it literally. This is why affirmations have the ability to help us transform ourselves. If we keep repeating positive phrases that are in the present tense, our brain begins to take the statement for fact and adjusts our awareness accordingly. We begin to notice the things, people, and situations that support this new belief about ourselves.

When affirmations don't work, it's usually because there is a hidden belief that counteracts the affirmation. That's why it's important to uncover what your beliefs are about intuition. You don't want anything hindering your ability to affirm your powerful intuitive skills.

Here are a few affirmations you might choose to use:

✳ I am highly intuitive.

✳ I receive intuitive information with ease.

✳ My intuition is always accurate and working for my highest good.

✳ I enjoy experiencing aha! moments and trust they always occur right when they're supposed to.

What are some affirmations you can repeat to yourself—with positive emotion—that will support your use of your intuition? Don't underestimate the power of this simple activity to help you make your intuition work for you.

Aha!

Chapter Four **Use Your Head**

While pursuing her acting career, sure that her big break was to come at any time, Mary Ann 'fell' into photography. What started out as a way to make a little money doing headshots for her friends for promoting their acting careers, turned into a successful business. In fact, Mary Ann's work became so sought-after and well-known that she found herself sitting in the office of the president of one of the largest talent agencies in the world. She couldn't believe it. Finally, her big break had come! Who cared if it was coming through her side job of photographing people—at least she had her shot.

As the president of the talent agency was marveling over the power of her photographs and her ability to reveal the spirit of the person being photographed, Mary Ann was trying to get his attention about her abilities as an actor. The president of the agency finally got *her* attention when he stated that he wanted to hire her to take the headshots of ALL of his agency's talent! Here it was—the phenomenal break she was looking for—only it was in a completely different field than she'd always pictured. Mary Ann was so sure her vision of accepting the Oscar for best performance by an actress was meant to come true that she almost missed out on a life-changing experience.

And then it happened. Mary Ann had an aha! moment. Everything seemed to slow down, her inner critic shut up (for a moment), and she felt peace and clarity come over her. What was she thinking? This was her calling. She needed to seize this opportunity. The rest is history. She's now a highly sought-after photographer, with her work featured in two books, including *Fearless Women*.

The Challenge and the Gift of Your Mental Channel of Knowing

Mary Ann experienced both the weakness and the strength of the mental channel of knowing. We can get fixated on things being a certain way and bring that perception (stemming from memories, beliefs, attitudes, and even wishful thinking) to all of our new experiences and ultimately miss the opportunities those new experiences have to offer. Even when we tell ourselves we're being objective, research suggests that's not possible.

Thankfully, Mary Ann had a brief moment in that high-powered meeting when she released her assumptions about what was meant to be. At that time, intuitive information was able to blend with some concrete facts—a big, fat contract for doing work that she considered play and the realization that business had been flowing to her from her photography with ease. Releasing resistance allows new information to come in, but you still use your mental channel of knowing to acknowledge and frame the information you receive.

Because of her strong vision of being an actor, Mary Ann needed some solid data to help her accept and move forward on her aha! moment. Clearly that data—in the form of a steadily building reputation and clientele—had been coming in for awhile, but she hadn't been ready to acknowledge it.

Ignorance Is Not Always Bliss

As Mary Ann let go of her resistance to what her intuition had been trying to tell her for the past year or more, she figuratively took out the ear plugs and 'heard' her calling. Research shows that we have an amazing ability to ignore what we do not want to know. Many times people will tell me that they're not intuitive and that they don't receive any intuitive clues or 'hits.' Rarely is this really true. Most of the time it's because the individual isn't paying attention; doesn't know what to look, listen, or feel for; or doesn't want to 'hear' or know what intuition is trying to tell them.

In *Awakening Intuition*, Dr. Schulz describes a condition called alexithymia where the wires in some areas of the brain are weak, crossed, or even 'cut.' The left hemisphere of individuals with this condition is so dominant that they deny the truth even when their bodies are acting in complete opposition to what they're saying. Dr. Schulz shares a story of a friend whose left hand automatically turned on the windshield wipers to deal with rain (knew the truth and handled it), at the same time she firmly stated that it wasn't going to rain and ruin their day of horseback riding![23]

Even if most of us don't suffer from alexithymia, we've been raised in a culture that glorifies the logic of the left hemisphere and continually reinforces its superiority. And some of us are wired to strongly prefer the way our left hemisphere processes information, so a little reinforcement of the strengths or superiority of left-hemisphere thinking makes perfect sense to us. But as we discussed in Chapter Three, we need to work from our wise mind which honors and incorporates the wisdom of both the right hemisphere and the left. Otherwise, we're likely to miss some valuable information. And, for most of us, moving into our wise mind means toning down the dominance of the left and opening up to the wisdom of the right hemisphere.

> This is the problem for people who live too much in the left hemisphere. Their powerful frontal lobes are always telling them to ignore what's coming from the right hemisphere. As they drown out any input from the right brain and the temporal lobe, these frontal lobes repeat, "You don't know that. You can't know that. That can't be." They thus inhibit the input of emotion, intuition, and body connection from the right hemisphere.[24]

A Very Brief Tour of Your Brain

When Dr. Schulz spoke of the frontal lobes, she was talking about the area in the front of your head that is considered the control center of your brain where free will or intentional action (versus instinctive response) arises, where coordination between other areas of the brain occurs, and where your inner control-freak and judge reside. You have two frontal lobes (one in each hemisphere of the brain), two temporal lobes (on each side, behind the frontal lobes), and two parietal lobes (behind the frontal lobes and above the temporal lobes). Finally, the occipital lobes are in the back of your brain.

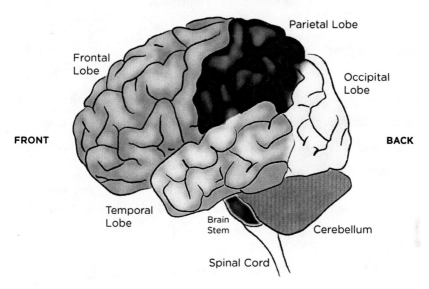

Regions of the Human Brain

Image Credit: www.medical-illustrations.ca

Whew! All of this describes only the cerebral or neocortex, the most recent evolution of your brain. Underneath this 'cap' of intelligence resides the mid-brain or the emotional brain, as it's involved in your emotional reactions to an event, in fight-or-flight decisions, and in ensuring the survival of your body. Daniel Goleman made the midbrain famous, especially the amygdalae (one in each hemisphere), with his book *Emotional Intelligence*. As we'll learn in the next chapter, it's unwise to underestimate the value and power of your emotions.

Beneath and behind the midbrain is the first brain (or reptilian brain) we evolved from. This part of your brain contains the brainstem and cerebellum. They control your physical actions (cerebellum) and the automatic functions that keep you alive (brainstem).

While there is no place where intuition or aha! moments officially reside or are generated from within the brain, some scientists believe intuitive information is processed via the temporal lobes which, among other things, are responsible for interpreting visual and auditory data and creating memories. Dr. Schulz considers the temporal lobes vital parts of the body's intuition network.

Both hemispheres of your brain are linked via the corpus callosum, which consists of millions of nerve fibers. Given all that I've shared about how different the two hemispheres are, you can imagine how critical your corpus callosum is to your ability to function effectively in the world.

Note: for a more detailed review of the areas of the brain and their vital role in your day-to-day life, please look at the list of recommended books in Appendix A.

Your Brain and the Energetic System of Knowing: A Hypothesis

While I'm obviously not a neuroscientist, I suspect that the mental channel of knowing is associated with the cerebral cortex, especially the frontal lobes. Perhaps the emotional channel of knowing sends information through the midbrain, the physical channel sends it through the first brain, and the spiritual channel sends information via the temporal lobe in the right hemisphere of the brain. This is talked about as the 'God Spot' after a study of epileptic patients revealed that a section of the temporal lobe was associated with religious or spiritual experiences. The reason an aha! moment is so powerful is likely that the brain is flooded with information (energy) from these different regions of the brain simultaneously.

While I wish I had a definitive answer for you—proven via testing— I'm not sure that really matters. What might some day be proven true for a group of test subjects, may not be true for you. The more scientists find out about the brain and how it works, the less we really know how each individual brain processes and interprets information. As I mentioned earlier, one of the most profound findings of neuroscience is that no two brains are wired the same way. Most of us might start out with similar hardware, located in similar spots within the brain. After that, our brains morph into the unique processing and thinking organs they are.

New Experiences: New Brain

Your experiences throughout your life color your perceptions and *change* the neural connections within your brain. After understanding that no two brains are wired exactly alike, the other profound discovery of neuroscience is the plasticity of the brain. We used to think that once we moved beyond adolescence, the vast majority of brain development was done, and it was pretty much downhill from then on. As the quote from Dr. Restak indicates, we now know that our brains keep learning, re-wiring, and re-wiring again until the day we die.

> We now recognize that our brain isn't limited by considerations that are applicable to machines. Thoughts, feelings, and actions, rather than mechanical laws, determine the health of our brain. Furthermore, we now know that the brain never loses the power to transform itself on the basis of experience, and this transformation can occur over very short intervals.[25]
>
> *Richard Restak, M. D.*

You See a Green Light, I See a Red Light (Or at Least a Yellow Caution)

Let's look at a possible scenario that shows the challenges your unique, changeable brain can create. Imagine that you're sitting in a meeting with your boss right now. Both of you are looking at the latest round of research on a potential new product, slated to launch in nine months. The data and the words on the paper are exactly the same, yet the two of you interpret them completely differently. Despite the obvious difference in rank and experience, your view that the data shows the product isn't ready to launch isn't necessarily wrong or stupid and your boss's view that "we're ready to roll" isn't necessarily right. You can't help but bring in all of your past experiences, beliefs, and attitudes into your review of the data. She can't either.

While reviewing the data about the new product—let's call it Product Wow—you and your boss can't help but reflect on the last product launch you experienced, the launch of Product Whoa. Your memories might be completely different, even though both of you were involved in the same product launch! Your boss vividly remembers the accolades she received for launching the product on time and for its impact on the bottom line last year. To her, 'whoa' means awesome and amazing. To you, on the other hand, just thinking about Product Whoa reminds you of the blistering negative comments you heard from product development for releasing the product too soon. For you, whoa means "Whoa, Nellie, slow down or stop." Both of you are right.

And, if different memories aren't enough to add to your unique perspective on the latest data, guess what? Research shows that we can reinvent memories to suit our needs. So your different memories of the launch of Product Whoa might not even be the 'real' memories.

For Goodness' Sake, I Know What I Experienced

When you think you've clearly remembered a past experience, think again.

Research indicates that you're just as likely to have created a new memory of the experience to fit your needs at the time of recollection. All of the studies I've read about involved having individuals write down a detailed account of where they were and what they were doing at the time they heard of some traumatic event, like the 9-11 disaster. Even only a few years later, when asked about where they were and what they were doing when they heard about the event, the individual will rarely remember it as they had written it. We re-write history to suit us. In one case, the individual saw his own written account and confirmed that it was his handwriting, but he still insisted that the written memory wasn't correct—his most recent recollection was.

So as you sit in your meeting with your boss reviewing data, you bring all that makes you unique into the analysis. Some of what you bring might be 'facts' with which others concur and some might be your own beliefs that arise out of skewed interpretations of events that no other person would or could validate as accurate. There is no one logical way to approach data and you can't be a dispassionate observer of anything, especially anything that you have a stake in. *Your* logical, reasoned analysis can lead to very different results than someone else's. Or, even if you reach the same conclusion, it will likely be based on unique interpretations of the different variables involved, which might come back to cause communication problems later.

The ability to think logically, to apply sound reason to a decision, and to go through a painstaking process of deduction is vital to successfully navigating through life and bringing creative ideas to life as products that get produced on time and on budget. But it is hardly the foolproof, superior way of processing information that it's deemed to be.

As we explore more in the next chapter on emotions, our system (I say system to represent your brain, body, and energy field) will do everything it can to not change, or remain at homeostasis. The brain, the heart, the emotions, the energy field, and all the cells that make up *you* all work together to keep you at your current chemical (and energetic) set point. And, your *thinking* is not immune to the needs of your system.

Honor Your Thoughts and Beliefs. But Act From Your Inner Guidance

Why would we be designed to be so biased and sometimes blind in our thinking and so driven by our chemistry? It makes no sense unless we really do have an inner guidance system that is highly attuned to who we are at any given moment and to what we can tolerate to think and to know. Maybe our brains aren't so haphazardly designed after all. Maybe all of the tricks our minds can play are designed to keep us safely in a zone until we're ready to jump to the next level. Then the aha! comes in to shift our energy.

Using our previous example of reviewing data with the boss about an upcoming product launch, this new understanding of how subtly we bring in our perspective and past into any review of data suggests that all involved need to be open to other perspectives. And the final decision needs to reflect a check-in with all four ways of knowing of the key decision-makers before jumping to the conclusion that your or your manager's analysis of the situation is correct.

If it's a matter of ignoring the truth (which is usually obvious to co-workers, friends, and family), then maybe we should trust that if our brain helps us ignore or deny something, we're simply not ready to hear or see it. Instead of seeing this as a flaw in your design after someone has pointed out what should have been obvious, have compassion for yourself and embrace that blind spot for the help it gave you. For example, perhaps you weren't meant to realize your husband was having an affair until the moment you did. You may have thought you should have figured it out sooner, but there could be many reasons why the timing wasn't right. Trust your innate wisdom to reveal to you what you need to know when you need to know it.

Going back to our photographer, Mary Ann, her strong mental picture of what she thought she wanted was valuable for many years in keeping her motivated. It guided her thoughts and her beliefs about who she was and what she was meant to do. However, that locked-in vision ultimately became a hindrance to seeing who she was truly meant to be. When you create a vision of what you want and hold an image of it, be willing to detach from the vision and be open to twists and turns that will lead you to what you're truly meant to do at this time in your life.

A Note On Finding Your Life Purpose

Sometimes people know as a child who and what they're meant to be for the rest of their lives. Some people don't figure it out until they're sixty-five. Others understand that their life is meant to include different phases of different missions or purposes. And, sadly, there are those people who are so locked into an image of the way it's supposed to be or the way they're supposed to find out what they're meant to do that they limp along in mediocre lives and miss the signs that have been there all along.

Trust that whenever your aha! moment about your ideal career or life purpose comes, it arrives exactly when it's supposed to. For whatever reason, you needed all of the experiences you had before to create the person you are at this moment to transform into the phenomenal person you are now being guided to become.

There are millions of photographers in the world today. Mary Ann's photography is unique because of who she is and who she thought she wanted to become.

Having spent so many years acting and pursuing her acting and stage career, she has a unique perspective looking through a lens that no other photographer has. Perhaps Mary Ann wasn't meant to 'see' the vision of herself as a world-renowned photographer until she was sitting in that office.

That's why the power of the intuitive energy was so strong and created the aha! just then. To believe otherwise is to waste precious energy—your most valuable resource—worrying about when, why, and how your big aha! is going to show up. Trust that you create the optimal time and scenario for your aha! moments to reveal themselves to you.

At the same time that you trust that aha! moments come exactly when they're supposed to, you can still do all that you can to encourage them to come often and clearly.

What do I mean by 'clearly?' Well, Mary Ann's insight into her calling or vocation could have simply been a thought in her head that she ignored. What made it so powerful was the sense of 'knowing' that came with the thought. It wasn't just an awareness of the idea, it was an understanding of the truth of the insight, and ultimately a knowing that resonated throughout her body and mind. It is the clarity that comes with an aha! that makes it so powerful and unique.

That clarity gives you the courage and confidence to step in a new direction, to make a change, no matter how small, that before the aha! moment you weren't willing to consider. The move or step seemed too drastic, scary, unsettling, risky, or frightening before. But once the 'knowing' settles in your bones, so to speak, your energy shifts and you can move in a new direction.

This energy shift is fragile and fluid at first. It hasn't 'locked in.' Remember, your body strongly prefers the status quo. When you have an aha!, you have an energy shift that makes it easier for you to move forward. However, this isn't foolproof. That's why people can take two steps forward, following their aha! insight, only to take three steps back and wind up stuck again.

Pay attention to your inner critic and your tendency to reach back toward the comfort of old thoughts, emotions, and behaviors. Make no judgment. This is simply your body's way of trying to stay at its old set point. Acknowledge that that's what those critical thoughts are trying to do and CHOOSE to ignore them. Create a vivid picture in your mind of the aha! moment or experience. Do this so that you can recall it at a moment's notice when you start to slide back to old behaviors. Let it be the beacon that it truly is to guide you in the direction that you're meant to go. How do you know if it's the right direction? It feels right. It feels good. It feels like a movement toward joy and toward what inspires you.

In Mary Ann's case, she'd spent a lot of time and energy on her dream of being an actor. She would not give it up lightly. Imagine if her intuition had told her before she was ready; that photography was her calling. She likely would have become frightened and walked away from photography for fear it would sabotage what she thought was her true dream.

Your soul sends you the aha! just when you're ready to heed it and most likely to act upon it and not before. Relax. Trust that the guidance will come when you're ready and open to it, and it will.

Acknowledge Your Brilliance and Your Blind Spots

In order to create the fertile ground for more aha! moments in your life, it's important to understand each of your channels of knowing and how you might be emphasizing one or two to the detriment of the others. We started with the mental channel of knowing, as it's the channel most of us in the Western world are comfortable with and usually trying to use to the exclusion of the others.

As you've seen in this chapter, your brain is a masterpiece, filled with knowledge and capabilities of which you have no conscious awareness. It's tailor-made to maximize your unique potential at any given moment. You are brilliant—no matter what anyone or any test ever told you. You are brilliant and your brilliance is unique to who you're meant to be and what you're meant to do in this world. But, that brilliance comes with a caution.

Your mental knowing or intellect is associated with your inner critic as well. And that inner critic's job is to keep you safely thinking, feeling, and doing the same old things. This part of you is your left brain's best friend, as it's not very comfortable with change either. If this is a highly developed part of you, you will likely be open to only a limited amount of possibilities and aha! moments. Why? Your left brain likes to run the thinking show and can't imagine any other way of discerning the rightness of a decision and could care less about emotional, spiritual, or physical ways of knowing.

Let's call this part of you 'LB' for short. LB *knows* it's superior at processing information and thinks its way of making a decision is the only way that counts. It tells itself and you that it's very rational and objective, bringing in all sorts of data and expert opinion. It will do all that it can to discredit any other forms of knowing, even knowing that brings up important personal beliefs and values.

While this part of us is critical to successfully maneuvering our way in this world and getting anything accomplished, it is ONLY one way of knowing—and, quite frankly, the least important way. Start seeing your mental intellect as only a part of you. It's not your soul or spirit. It's not the only way you receive information. If you think of LB as the most amazing computer, then you begin to see LB as the incredible tool and partner it is—but it is not you. So, if mental knowing or intellect does not reflect all of you, why wouldn't you explore the other forms of knowing?

Develop, engage, and enjoy your left brain's ability to categorize, process, analyze, and evaluate information in order to deduct an answer, but don't blindly follow its reasoning at the expense of your other sources of information and knowing.

Inspired Questions, Actions, and Leaps

✳ Think about some of your most powerful memories. Now consider that they might not be completely accurate or true. In the case of positive memories, that's not a big deal. In the case of negative memories, you can use this information to reframe or adjust the memories you had. Don't let your memories drive you. Use them.

✳ What's your vision of your ideal career or life? Do you have one?

✳ Is it time to update your vision? Has any new information come in to adjust your thinking?

✳ You might be doing a lot less thinking than you think. Research suggests that many times your nonconscious mind makes the decision and seconds later, you consciously think you thought up the answer. This is great for quickly making decisions, but is also a caution to be sure you're as aware as you can possibly be about what your beliefs are and how they drive you. Perhaps this is why Socrates' exhortation to 'know thyself' has stood the test of time. What are you doing to make sure you really know yourself and what drives you?

....

Need An Aha! Moment? Try This!

Do Nothing. Because intuitive messages are usually delivered via subtle nudges (gut feelings, goosebumps, and so on), soft sounds or inner voices, or images that pop into our heads while daydreaming, many of us miss them. We're so focused on our immediate problems, rehashing the past, or worrying about the future that we miss all of the inner guidance being sent to us. The simplest way to handle this is to give yourself permission to sit quietly and wait for the answer to come.

I confess, this is something I find challenging. I'm constantly coaxing myself into meditating and taking quiet time. One way I get around this is to ask myself a question and set the timer for ten to fifteen minutes to wait for the answer. If I'm feeling particularly restless, I will pose the same question to myself, but this time I'll play a few rounds of solitaire on the computer. The game keeps my left brain busy and allows my intuition to speak to me. Some of the most powerful guidance I've received has come to me this way.

The point is to honor yourself and your ways of receiving information. To 'do nothing' may look different for you than for me. Maybe sitting on a park bench looking at the sunset is your way of doing nothing. The whole idea is to simply cut down on the noisy distractions (both inner and outer) and allow your intuition to communicate with you. Even five minutes of dedicated silence at the beginning or end of your day can have a profound effect on your ability to access your intuition and generate aha! moments.

Aha!

Chapter Five **Listen to Your Heart**

Luisa and her husband had been trying to have children for years. They'd been to doctors and tried all the suggested procedures, medicines, and prayers they could. They'd talked about adoption, but Luisa really wanted to have the experience of pregnancy and giving birth.

During a workshop I offered at her company, I had the participants, including Luisa, think of a question they wanted their intuition or nonconscious mind to help them with. Luisa asked whether it was time to let go of the dream of having a baby and proceed with adoption.

With her question clear in her mind, Luisa, along with her peers, walked over to a table to pick up one of approximately fifty pictures cut out from magazines. The pictures had a piece of yellow paper backing them and were turned over, so participants couldn't see which picture they were grabbing.

As instructed, Luisa used her intuition to pick the 'right' picture, turned it over to see the image, and quickly (without *thinking* about it) discerned what the image had to say about her question.

Like many people doing this exercise, Luisa was surprised to experience an aha! moment of clarity. The image brought tears to her eyes, as the message her soul seemed to be giving her via the image was clear: "Let go and proceed with adoption." While her friends who sat near her didn't understand how she could be that clear from the picture—they didn't get that message for her when they looked at it—Luisa had a calm, albeit sad, certainty about it.

For Luisa, it was the sense of peace that came from looking at the picture that told her what her soul had likely known for awhile. Images can be a rich source of intuitive wisdom, as they require us to get out of our logical, analytical left brain and into the world of metaphor and symbols that our intuitive right brain loves.*

When we release our resistance to what our intuition can tell us, we're open to the intuitive associations that pop into our heads when we gaze at a picture picked 'randomly.' (Who knows? If everything is energy and each picture has its own vibration, then isn't it possible that the picture *picks you* based upon the vibration of the question you're asking? Just a thought).

The Power of Emotion

I don't know about you, but I find it easy to get confused about how to make the most, in a positive sense, of my emotions. Despite the growing body of work on the subject of emotional intelligence, there is still a lot of misunderstanding about what emotions are and how powerful we are once we understand and harness the energy and wisdom of our emotions.

When I speak of 'Emotional Energy,' I literally mean the energy that you can feel within and without you when you attune yourself to it. As you probably have experienced, positive emotions have a higher, lighter vibration and negative emotions have a lower, more dense vibration.

---

* People have asked me what the image was that had such an impact on Luisa. I honestly don't remember which of about fifty images she selected; however, I believe it was a landscape that said 'barren' to her. I've lost touch with her and don't know whether or not she and her husband have adopted or even given birth to a child. (Something that seems to happen some times after couples let go of the expectation of having a baby).

Can you discern what a range of emotions feel like to you? What does peace *feel* like? Do you know? Can you recognize it when it comes? If someone asks you "what does your heart tell you to do?" can you answer them? If you find it difficult to answer these questions, it will be hard to register true intuitive information or aha! moments. You may think that's funny, but sometimes we can get so wrapped up in our heads or be so afraid of emotions that we have a hard time discerning the particular emotion we're feeling in any given moment.

My first true understanding that I was disconnected and blocking my awareness of many of my emotions came when I picked up Gary Zukav and Linda Francis' book, *The Heart of the Soul.* While I had heard about emotional awareness and intelligence while still working in my corporate job, I was so disconnected that I assumed because I was *emotional*, I understood and was aware of my emotions. Boy, was I wrong, and Zukav and Francis were the ones who made that crystal clear for me.

The truth is if your emotional channel of knowing is so blocked that you don't really know what emotions you're experiencing at any given time (and why), then you can't fully experience aha! moments. You miss the signals your emotions send—a vital part of an aha! experience. Zukav and Francis helped me to realize that I was not alone in my misunderstanding about emotions and clarified for me the power that comes from getting in touch with and making friends with your emotions.

> Learning to experience emotions is one of the most difficult tasks that can be undertaken. Many people do not know that they are angry, even when rage flows through them like a river. Some do not know that they are grieving, even when sorrow is the only sun that rises for them in the morning. Most people think of themselves as experiencing emotions only

when powerfully emotional currents erupt through
their lives, disturbing routines devoted to activities,
accomplishments, or survival.[26]

What Message Are Your Emotions Sending You?

Your emotions are 'currents of energy' running through your
system and wonderful signals about how closely you're aligned with
your soul or Higher Self. As Zukav and Francis point out, "your most
painful emotions show you what you are most resistant to changing."[27]
Notice that this statement is about you. Nowhere is there a reference to
other people or situations that might 'cause' your emotional reaction.
Every time we experience a negative emotion, we are signaling that we're
reacting (resisting) to something in fear. That's powerful information.
Of course, so is joyful exuberance.

The same exercise with the pictures described at the beginning of
the chapter was done as part of a right-brain 'warm-up' for a group
of senior executives before they began participating in a series of
brainstorming activities. Janice, the consultant leading this project,
participated in the group exercises too. For the 'pick a picture' exercise,
Janice asked her nonconscious mind to help her discern whether she
and her husband should purchase a condo on the beach in Port Aransas,
Texas as a rental property and for weekend getaways.

Janice gave a big whoop of joy when she turned over her picture and
saw a couple holding hands on a gorgeous beach, kicking their feet up
(wearing flippers) as they were wading into the water to go snorkeling.
(Clearly this was a vacation getaway advertisement she was looking at).
Janice's reaction was so positive that I don't think there was any immediate
sense of peace! That came later. However, her soul was clearly telling her—
via her emotions—that it was most definitely on board with the plan.

Learning to experience emotions is one of the most difficult tasks that can be undertaken. Many people do not know that they are angry, even when rage flows through them like a river.

Gary Zukav and Linda Francis

Navigating Life Via Emotions

Your thoughts affect your emotions and thus your vibration at any given moment. Remember the radio antenna example—think of yourself as an antenna sending and receiving signals. If your frequency doesn't match signals buzzing around you, you'll never pick them up. So your thoughts and emotions affect what you are attracting (or repelling) to you. It makes sense, then, that your emotions serve as a clear indicator of whether the thoughts you are thinking are in line with your soul or Higher Self. The more aligned the thoughts, the more positive the emotion. The less aligned the thoughts, the more negative the emotion.

For the vast majority of us who have brains that bounce from one thought to the other in an unending inner dialogue, the idea of trying to pay attention to and alter our thoughts into more loving, supportive, or positive ones is overwhelming at the least. That's why focusing on your emotions makes more sense. While many of us can have trouble initially registering what the emotion we're feeling in the moment is, as noted above, it's a lot easier to develop sensitivity to your emotions than it is to monitor your thoughts (you'd probably go crazy trying!)

Knowing that your thoughts lead to emotions, you can move in the direction of more positive emotions by deliberately changing your thoughts. Think about all of the times you tell yourself a story about why someone hasn't returned a phone call, answered an e-mail, or followed up on something you've contacted them about. We all have that inner critic that can play tricks on us. One of the best things we can do when we can feel our thoughts pushing us into fear, sadness, guilt, anger, or any other negative emotion is to stop and ask ourselves 'is that really true?' Spiritual leader Byron Katie has a series of four questions, including 'Is it true?,' that she calls 'The Work.'[28] When you do The Work, you halt the negative story running rampant in your head and can then shift your thinking and begin to move forward or beyond the negative thought loop that had you in its grip.

Clearly it's important to pay attention to your emotions in any given moment and to guide yourself to a more positive perspective about any situation. However, that's easier said than done when we have a strong belief or memory associated with the situation. At least that's been my experience.

Attack of the Pain-Body!

At the end of June 2008, I was talking with a friend who was visiting from out of town. She mentioned that she had read and been positively affected by Eckhart Tolle's book, *A New Earth*. The only thing she wasn't sure she got or agreed with was this spiritual teacher's discussion of the 'pain-body.' I mentioned that I hadn't read that far in the book, but remembered his discussion of it in his other book, *The Power of Now*.

That night I couldn't stop thinking about that brief segment of our conversation and felt compelled to pick up my copy of *A New Earth*. I looked in the Table of Contents for the chapter on the pain-body and immediately flipped to it. Tolle describes the pain-body as "an accumulation of old emotional pain" carried within each of our energy fields. As I read the words, I *felt* a sense of peace and relief at the disappearance of some anxiety I had been feeling about my finances that I now understood came from experiences I had with money as a young adult—and my eyes filled with tears.

Even after my aha! moment, I confess I felt a bit silly about believing in this thing called a pain-body. I could understand why my friend didn't buy into the idea of the pain-body. While creating a vivid picture that my right brain loved, Tolle's further description of the pain-body as taking over my physical body sounded a bit like a B movie monster terrorizing me.

The usual pattern of thought creating emotion is
reversed in the case of the pain-body, at least initially.
Emotion from the pain-body quickly gains control of
your thinking, and once your mind has been taken over
by the pain-body, your thinking becomes negative.[29]

The truth is, Tolle's description was a little hard for my left brain
and inner critic to swallow in the light of day. Thankfully, just as doubts
were setting in, I was inspired to pick up another book that I've had for
awhile, but never finished, *Evolve Your Brain* by Joe Dispenza. Again,
I found the chapter I thought I was looking for, started reading, and
was blown away with how beautifully Dr. Dispenza gave a more scientific explanation for the pain-body (a term he never used, but which I
believe is a left-brain match for Tolle's more right-brain description).

What's so amazing about this story is the information I learned
to help me deal with my struggles with trusting that the money will
come is a perfect fit for this chapter as well. I had started on the chapter, but wasn't particularly happy with the way it was going. When all
of these aha's unfolded in a matter of days, it became clear to me that
for all of us to truly understand and make the most of the power of our
emotional energy, we needed to better understand it.

As I flipped back and forth between both books, I realized that
while each was brilliant in its own way, for many people a blend of
both (I like to think of it as a more whole-brain version) would be truly
transformational. Please note that this is my interpretation. Neither
author has been privy to my thinking and so may completely disagree.
However, I hope that at minimum I will have inspired you to read or
re-read these books with a new mind.

Your Emotions Are a Chemical Cocktail

In his book *Evolve Your Brain*, author Joe Dispenza (featured in the movie *What the Bleep Do We Know?*) takes us on an in-depth journey into the power of our brain and internal chemistry to help us heal and transform our lives. With his own improbable recovery from a terrible car accident, this chiropractor began a lifelong study of why some people experience what many of us would describe as miraculous recoveries from debilitating, and in many cases, life-threatening illnesses or accidents.

As part of his research, Dr. Dispenza discovered studies that proved that our thoughts and emotions are linked and create a chemical cycle within our bodies. For example, when I think a negative thought like, "If this house doesn't sell soon, I won't be able to pay my bills," that thought has its own chemical cocktail associated with it and sends a signal to my body to create a matching emotional chemical cocktail, so my body will feel anxious, worried, fearful, or depressed. The emotional feeling (energy) created and expressed in my body will now send back a signal to my brain, which will in turn create a matching thought to go with the feeling. So now I'm in a vicious cycle of thoughts and feelings matching each other to keep me feeling fearful! Doesn't this sound suspiciously like that B movie character, the pain-body?

What's even more bizarre is that research shows that, as chemical beings, our body gets used to a certain chemical mix or cocktail. It is designed to want to stay at that level or set point, so it will influence the brain to think thoughts or to remember experiences that will keep us at that emotional level.

> Every time we fire a thought in our brain, we make chemicals, which produce feelings and other reactions in the body. Our body grows accustomed to the level

of chemicals coursing through our bloodstream, surrounding our cells, and bathing our brain. Any interruption in the regular, consistent, and comfortable level of our body's chemical makeup will result in discomfort. **We will do nearly everything we can, both consciously and subconsciously, based on how we feel, to restore our familiar chemical balance.**[30]

When we are locked in a cycle of thoughts and emotions, our body will do all that it can to keep the cycle going. An aha! moment breaks that cycle, so you experience a shift in both your thoughts and emotions. However, it's now easy to understand why we can slip back into the same old routine or patterns—basically ignoring what our aha! experience gave us in terms of next steps, clarity, or guidance—if we don't stay vigilant in creating a new, more positive chemical set point within our body.

When you are in the midst of trying to solve a problem, move in a new direction, or come up with a new creative idea, your brain and body might be getting in the way because of where you are emotionally at the time. Even if you don't consider yourself 'emotional,' that doesn't mean that you don't have your own emotional set point. This is why some people are more inclined to see the cup half-full and others are more inclined to see the cup half-empty—their emotional 'cocktail' is driving their thinking.

All our emotional attitudes—ones we may believe are caused by something outside of us—are not only the result of how we perceive reality based on how we are wired, but also of how much we are addicted to how we want to feel.[31]

As Dr. Dispenza states, you may not want to think of it this way, but it's true—your body becomes addicted to feeling a certain way and it will do whatever it can to influence your thinking, so that you will continue to feel the way it's used to. Your body does not determine what is a healthy set point (more positive) versus an unhealthy set point (more negative). It simply wants to remain in balance wherever it currently is at the time. For example, if you walk into a brainstorming session at the office feeling angry at this waste of time because you've been angry all day, your body is going to do its best to have you keep thinking angry thoughts, so it can continue to feel angry.

Now, if nothing in your day is helping to feed the emotional state you've been in, your body will call up memories that make you think the thoughts it needs to feel the emotions it desires! In turn, you will feel compelled to seek out a situation that will help you maintain your chemical balance.

If that jerk you had to deal with in purchasing is no longer at the company, you'll find another 'jerk' to enable you to feel the frustration or anger you're used to feeling at the end of your work day. Worst case, you'll find yourself wondering what happened to that jerk and recalling all of the bad experiences that occurred with him or her. In a matter of moments you've got yourself worked up to an angry state and now your body is satisfied!

Knowing all of this, the idea of a pain-body starts to make sense, doesn't it? In *A New Earth*, Eckhart Tolle talks about the need for us to become conscious of who we really are (*not* our thoughts or emotions) in order to raise the consciousness of this planet and to improve our own lives. He points out that we are not our thoughts and emotions, but the 'Being witness' to those thoughts and emotions. The body's addiction to stored-up memories of pain—which he describes as an energy field that is addicted to negativity or unhappiness—is not us.

When you can detach from and be a witness to all of the valuable messages your emotions are sending you (both the positive and the negative), you're more likely to relax, pay attention, and receive the essential communication that comes to you via this powerful channel of knowing. And, most important, you'll be able to have more compassion for yourself when you do get taken over by your pain-body, or your body demands an emotional chemical cocktail fix.

You are not your emotions or your emotional responses. But they certainly have a lot to share with you if only you will take the time to listen and heed their message. The key is to pay attention to how you're feeling at any given time and to ask yourself why. Take responsibility for the emotions you feel. They're a message for you and no one else. Remember, it's just energy. And energy is always moving. Receive the message, then let the energy go or flow.

Pick Up the Signals

Your Emotional Channel of Knowing is a wonderful source of valuable information to guide you toward what serves you and away from what doesn't. It's also able to help you steer through life by enabling you to pick up the emotions of others. Some people—perhaps you're one of them—are able to literally feel or sense the emotional energy that has been flowing in a room when they walk into it.

Have you ever walked into a room and sensed that an argument had taken place there before? Depending upon how sensitive you are, you can actually pick up on emotional energy left behind months and even years before. It is a tangible force that flows through and around you.

Of course empathy is that ability to acknowledge others' emotions and adjust your communication and actions accordingly. Even though people's emotions are their responsibility, not yours, connecting with them requires acknowledging and being sensitive to their emotions. When your Emotional Channel of Knowing is open and clear, you can easily pick up on the energetic, physical, and verbal signals of how someone is feeling. When you're only in your Mental Channel of Knowing, you're aware only of the specific actions or words you witness, not the underlying emotion behind those actions or words.

When you're open and paying attention, your emotions and the emotions of others provide you with a rich source of information. Keeping your channel open is simple, but not always easy.

∗ Pay attention to what you're feeling at any given moment.

∗ Acknowledge the emotion. Is it more positive or negative? Can you name it? While fear about something usually underlies all negative emotions, it can be helpful to get a sense of whether it's a feeling of frustration, anger, or anxiety, for example.

∗ Try to discern what thoughts or actions are causing the emotion. Go back to the thoughts you were thinking before you noticed the emotion.

∗ Use that information to determine what would need to change, starting with your power to change your thoughts—to talk yourself into a better feeling. For example, you might gently challenge yourself about a statement such as "I'll never be able to accomplish that." Is it true? (Check out the work of Byron Katie. Her series of simple questions are a powerful way to release you from the trap of negative mental chatter).

∗ Take appropriate action in changing thoughts, getting more information, or taking action steps.

✳ Remember that the emotion (positive and negative) is energy. Consciously release it via physical activity, writing in a journal, or talking with a close friend or trained therapist. Or, if positive, reinforce the emotion via visualizing whatever generated that emotion, sharing the positive experience with friends, or using a fist pump or other physical movement to remember it, but let the emotion flow through you.

✳ Once you're in a positive frame of mind, pay attention to the emotional energy around you and affecting the people you're with.

✳ Remember, other people's emotional reactions are not about you. They're about their beliefs, their emotional set point, or their pain-body.

✳ Empathize with others as needed, but let their emotions flow through and not stick to you.

Inspired Questions, Actions, and Leaps

What do you think your emotional set point typically is on the scale below? Spend a day paying attention to the emotions that are most prevalent in you throughout the day.

✳ Joy-Freedom-Peace

✳ Love

✳ Confidence-Anticipation-Excitement

✳ Acceptance-Hope

✳ Boredom

✳ Frustration

✳ Anxiety-Overwhelm

✳ Rage-Anger

✳ Desire-Addiction-Greed-Jealousy

✳ Fear

✳ Grief-Sadness-Depression

✳ Apathy-Despair-Hopelessness-Powerlessness

✳ Shame-Guilt

Now notice the thoughts you typically think that keep you feeling that way. Practice talking yourself into the next level up.[32] For example, if you've spent the last week with an emotional set point ranging from angry to frustrated because you can't let go of being passed over for a promotion again, you probably want to move toward a more life-enhancing set point of 'accepting-hopeful-encouraged.'

Acknowledge your anger and disappointment, then remind yourself of the positive feedback you received from those who interviewed you, the awareness of your strong potential for the other position coming open next month, and so on. Or, you might tell yourself that this was really good news, as it provides the impetus to actively search for a better job. The point is to consciously move toward a healthier emotional set point.

After playing with this concept for awhile, try looking at the major areas of your life. You likely have a different set point for work, family, romance, finances, and so on.

Do you sometimes get so caught up in the pros and cons of a decision that you lose awareness of how you truly feel about the options? If so, flip a coin. Break the decision down into 'yes' and 'no' choices. Flip a quarter. Heads is yes and tails is no. I don't recommend this as a way to make a decision, but as a way to get at how you *feel* about the choices.

For example, if heads/yes is 'I move to Austin' and tails/no is 'I stay in Seattle,' then when you see George Washington's head, notice what the immediate feeling is (don't think about it). Your reaction reflects how you truly feel about a possible move to Austin. That's exactly what I did and I ended up moving to Austin within seven months of doing the coin toss!

....

Need An Aha! Moment? Try This!

An Image is Worth One Thousand Words. Because the left hemisphere tends to dominate the right, you can help your intuition along by doing activities that make no logical sense and therefore shut down the left hemisphere of your brain. Betty Edwards talks about this in her acclaimed book, *Drawing on the Right Side of the Brain*. Edwards explains that we all have an ability to draw, but that most of us have let our left hemisphere so dominate our thinking that we get in the way of allowing the image to transfer from our brain to our hands.[33]

Similarly, we may be so focused on logically thinking our way to a solution or creative idea that we can't 'hear' our intuition. One way to get out of your left brain is to use random photos or images to jog your intuition.

While it may seem ludicrous, using a random photo from a magazine or a card from a tarot deck to help you find the answer to a question allows your intuition to speak. Because this activity makes no sense to your left brain, it's at a loss for a moment—only a moment. The trick is to pay attention to the first thoughts or images that pop into your head when you look at the image.

Another option is to take a moment and look about your office, rest your eyes on an item or photo, and ask yourself what that item might have to say about the challenge you're facing. Remember that your right brain is visual and tends to let the left brain lead. Doing something this abstract and ridiculous gets your dominant, verbal left brain out of the way and lets the right, intuitive brain 'speak' to you.

Aha!

Chapter Six **Expand Your Physical Awareness**

It was happening again! Diane (her real name) felt her jaw tighten and her breathing become labored. Seconds later, everything returned to normal. Whew! When she thought about it, Diane realized this intense, scary combination of difficulty breathing and tension in her jaw had been happening off and on over the past six or seven months, with increasing regularity. And, if she wasn't imagining things, these episodes were lasting longer each time. "What's wrong?" she wondered.

She couldn't identify what was causing these scary episodes, but Diane *knew* something wasn't right. Diane started with her family doctor. Her physician knew about the demands of her job with an airline and told her, "It's just stress. You've got a stressful job, Diane. And you're always telling me that you've got too many family and work commitments."

On Diane's second visit to her physician, she received a prescription for anti-anxiety medication. That didn't *feel* right to Diane, but at this point, she was open to trying anything. Diane didn't notice any difference, but kept taking the pills. She decided to try a dentist. Maybe the tense jaw was due to a dental problem. No luck. The dentist confirmed that wasn't it.

While all of this was going on, Diane decided to take advantage of an extended leave of absence program her company offered. The downside of participating in the program was her health insurance premium would jump significantly. She talked it over with her husband and came close to canceling her existing policy with full benefits and buying cheaper insurance for limited coverage. At the last minute, she decided to keep her policy and pay the higher premium.

The insurance decision behind her, Diane refocused on her health. Her frustration about not being able to figure out what was going on intensified. She went back to her doctor. She heard the same explanation and wasn't satisfied. Then it came time to take a big trip out to California the family had been planning all summer.

At the last minute, Diane called her mother-in-law and said, "We're not coming. The trip's cancelled. I'm not feeling up to it." Two days later, Diane told her husband, "Something's wrong with me. I've got to see another doctor." She felt compelled to see a cardiologist. Diane immediately thought of the cardiologist who had spoken a few months earlier at a charitable function she attended. She concluded he must be 'good' if he was on the speaking circuit, so Diane called his office and was able to get in to see him. After a battery of tests, the cardiologist said, "Yes, I may know what's wrong with you. First, though, I need you to go to a cardiac care center for some specific tests that we can't do in this office and that aren't available in Austin."

Remember that decision about the insurance? Well, it certainly was a blessing, as the insurance company covered all of her expenses. She checked to see which cardiac care centers the insurance company would cover and found one in Houston, only a two-and-a-half-hour drive away. Within the week, Diane and her husband were in Houston for her tests.

As soon as the tests were completed, Diane was admitted into the hospital without delay. Her arteries were 90 percent blocked and required immediate surgery for her to avoid a deadly heart attack.

If Diane hadn't trusted her 'gut,' it would have been easy to ignore the messages her body was sending her that she desperately needed help. No one else, even her family physician, took her worries seriously. She did. She listened to the wisdom of her body and got the care she needed.

Diane didn't have one big aha! moment that led her immediately to a cardiologist. But she did have a series of intuitive insights (including the decision to renew her insurance) that led to a strong knowing just before the scheduled trip to California. Once she'd made the decision to cancel the family vacation, her confidence in her intuition grew. And, only two days later, the idea to see a cardiologist popped into her head.

Diane never forgot the power of her intuition, especially when it came to her body. And her faith in her intuition was to be tested again. Only a year after her heart surgery, Diane developed severe pain in her leg. She was afraid it might have something to do with her heart, so she went to her cardiologist. Thankfully, there was nothing wrong with her heart. But the doctor did suggest that she see another physician. When she called the office to make an appointment, she was told she'd have to wait three weeks to see the doctor.

As she drove home in tears and pain, Diane turned the car around and went to her new family physician. She told the front desk that she didn't have an appointment, but wanted to briefly talk with the doctor. She spoke with the doctor, who thankfully took her pain seriously. Her physician promised to call her that evening with a recommendation. After the promised phone call that night, Diane had the name of a vascular (vein) specialist who would fit her in the next day.

Once again, Diane's intuition saved her. She had one dozen blood clots in her leg from sitting for so long on a flight from Alaska a few days earlier! If she hadn't seen the doctor quickly, she could have died from the blood clots. Needless to say, Diane now makes every effort to stay in tune with her body.

Pay attention. That's the message of Diane's story. Your body contains and has access to a wealth of wisdom about your health, your work, your relationships, and much, much more. We are only just beginning to understand and open up to the language of our bodies, but the reality is that each body is unique. Yours will communicate to you in a way that best fits with who you are, how you prefer to learn or receive information, and how you best process that information.

Listen to Your Heart

Scientists are constantly learning and revealing the intelligence of our cells, the messages contained in our energy fields, and the wisdom that our bodies are able to energetically pick up and communicate to us. The scientific team at the Institute of HeartMath is quite familiar with the intelligence and critical role the body plays in communication. In particular, their research shows that the heart is so much more than an organ pumping blood and life through our bodies.

Your heart is your electromagnetic center of your body (five thousand times stronger than the brain's magnetic field), has its own brain (there's even a new branch of science called neurocardiology), and is in constant communication with your brain and the rest of your body. Research suggests the heart also plays a role in receiving intuitive information (even before it reaches the brain) and processing emotions.[34]

If you miss the signals your emotions try to send you, your body, in particular your heart, will reinforce the message. Research shows that when your heart is in coherence (rhythm), your ability to learn, manage stress, and receive intuitive information increases.

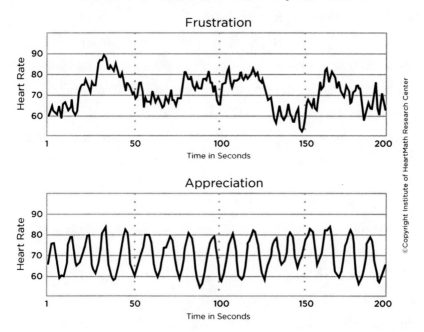

The Effect of Emotions on Heart Rhythm Patterns

The chart above shows the dramatically different effect two emotions have on your heart's rhythmic activity. Interestingly enough, further research shows that when you consciously make an effort to visualize the emotion of appreciation and imagine breathing it in, you can quickly change your heart's rhythm back to a more positive, coherent pattern. The Institute of HeartMath offers proven, quick tools anyone can use to bring themselves back into coherence (see Appendix B).

Now imagine that you need to make a decision, and you're trying to discern the right next step. Consider the possibility that your heart's rhythmic activity can tell you what direction to go in. If choice number one generates the same pattern as the emotion of appreciation, then put that at the top of your list of options. If choice number two generates the same pattern as the emotion of frustration, pick option number one.

Sound far-fetched? Well, consider this.

If Diane had been working with a medical intuitive, there would have been no 'push' to get cared for because he or she would have been able to look right 'through' Diane and pick up on the energy imbalance associated with blocked arteries. She might also have learned about any emotional issues that could be affecting her health. While many people still roll their eyes in disbelief of the idea of medical intuition, it's hard to discount the work of someone who is both a neuropsychiatrist and neuroscientist, and educated at Brown University and Boston University.

What the Heck Is a Medical Intuitive?

Mona Lisa Schulz, M.D., Ph.D., is a known medical intuitive. She can be on the phone with you, thousands of miles away, and energetically scan your body and tell you what you need to pay attention to or what is out of whack in your body. Importantly, Dr. Schulz, like another famous medical intuitive, Caroline Myss, does not seek to expand her medical intuitive practice. She'd rather train you to tap into the wisdom of your intuition and body.

As with the Emotional Channel of Knowing, most of us are so stuck in our heads and internal mental chatter that we can't begin to heed the messages from our body—from our Physical Channel of Knowing. We don't notice the emotions or thoughts that led to the discomfort or we attribute the irritation to indigestion, sleeping funny, or overdoing it. Eventually those aches and pains turn into a stop-you-in-your-tracks illness. And, even then, many of us would rather assume it's a random unlucky break, and take a pill to get over it.

But, as Dr. Schulz knows, your body's fluctuations in health are anything but random. They are a signal that something is out of whack in your life. Research shows the havoc negative emotions can have on us if we 'stuff' them or don't flush them out of our system. If you don't catch the message of a negative emotion early on, it will manifest in a disruption in the functioning of some part of your body.

> You can learn to understand the language your own body uses to communicate to you the needs and wants you are fulfilling or failing to fulfill. I'm talking not just about physical needs but about emotional needs as well, because the language of our bodies is actually part of the larger language of intuition and the soul, part of the intuition network, broadcasting vital information about our lives as a whole.[35]

This isn't a call to blame yourself for every illness or accident that befalls you. Sometimes things just happen, including a cross-wiring in the body. With a healthy inner critic, it's tempting to either take on blame for every ache and pain or to completely throw this idea of a connection between thoughts, emotions, and illness out the window.

Like the idea of operating from wise mind for processing information, consider a healthy blend of being inquisitive about what thoughts and emotions *might* have influenced or encouraged an illness and trusting yourself when it feels to you like there's no other meaning that you were just unlucky.

While I hope you'll never be called upon to consider what the emotional blocks are that might have led to (or helped along) a serious disease, I encourage you to become fluent with the relationship between blocked or buried emotions and illness. At minimum, open up to the idea that your body is a conduit for receiving information and guidance. Consider the possibility that your own body—like your emotions—will give you clear signals when you're making a decision aligned with your

Higher Self and when you're making a decision that is not in your best interest.

In the case of Diane, her body kept sending her signals about her illness. Sometimes those signals were the symptoms and the increased severity of those symptoms. Sometimes those signals were *feelings* of 'something is wrong.'

Heed the Messages Your Body Sends You

I first became open to the idea of my body communicating to me ten years ago via Louise Hay's small book, *Heal Your Body*. In it, this inspiring metaphysician and founder of Hay House Publishing would list an ailment or body part and the possible corresponding mental/ emotional issue associated with that illness or situation. I didn't really take it too seriously for awhile, but eventually started to check it out every time I had an ache, pain, or illness. I was amazed at how the symptoms would ease once I'd explored the possible emotional cause.

Yes, I know that's not scientific research, but it was enough (combined with what I'd begun to understand about energy and the intelligence of our cells) to convince me to 'pay attention.' Perhaps it was easy for me to finally be open to the idea of the body communicating through aches and pains because I'd just read *Power Versus Force* by David R. Hawkins, M.D., Ph.D. This book caused the aha! moment that launched Inspired Leap.

My Life-Changing Aha! Moment

I was sitting on a chair, in the middle of reading Hawkins' book when he talked about sharing the profound power of muscle testing with the business world with Sam Walton. I sat up abruptly and felt chills up and down my spine. The message from my body was loud and clear: 'Pay attention' it said.

You can learn to understand the language your own body uses to communicate to you the needs and wants you are fulfilling or failing to fulfill.

Mona Lisa Schulz, M.D., Ph.D.

As I continued to read the chapter on possibilities for using muscle testing in business, I realized that I wanted to bring enlightened ideas and principles (whether from quantum physics, leading-edge neuroscience, or spiritual teachings) to the business world. My business has evolved over the years, but it was my fascination and awe over the power of our bodies to discern the truth of a statement that sparked my new direction in life.

Your Muscles Know

Are you familiar with muscle testing, or kinesiology? It's simply a method of using the strength or weakness of a muscle (usually an arm held out to your side) after making a statement or holding a product. For example, a naturopath might use muscle testing to determine what food items you might be allergic to or have some toxicity to. If appropriate, further blood tests might be done, but the muscle testing can be a first line of discernment.

For example, almost anyone holding a packet of artificial sweetener next to their heart with one hand, putting their other arm straight out to their side, and trying to hold the arm 'strong' while a second person tried to lightly push the arm down would be unable to do so. All it takes is a light push and the body goes 'weak,' signaling that artificial sweetener is harmful or 'negative' for the body.

Hawkins' more than twenty years of research showed that muscle testing can be used to accurately determine the truth of any statement, whether it be about oneself, a loved one, or a complete stranger.

Like Hawkins' studies, the work of Bruce Lipton (*The Biology of Belief*) and Candace Pert (*Molecules of Emotions*) and many others is revealing the innate intelligence of every cell of our being, how thoughts and emotions affect our cells, and the ability of our cells to pick up on the questions we're asking, tapping into the intelligence of stored memories and the energy fields around us to provide us the answers we seek.

According to Dr. Hawkins (and his review of data from the world of quantum physics), following a specific kinesiological testing procedure (that he used for all of his research), virtually everything past and present is knowable to any of us! And that "one's every thought and action leave an indelible trace forever in the universe."[36]

While this can seem far-fetched, when you again consider that every thought and emotion has its own vibration that can be picked up throughout the universe and that the thoughts and emotions do not die, then this really isn't far-fetched at all. A bit disconcerting perhaps, but not unbelievable.

As noted earlier, many naturopaths, chiropractors, and other 'alternative' healers are very familiar with muscle testing and use it in their practices. There are even some traditionally trained physicians who are open to and comfortable using it as well. At minimum, I urge you to 'play' with muscle testing and consider the possibility that your muscles (body) have access to all of the wisdom you need.

It would be nice if muscle testing could predict the future, but alas, we all have free will and can thus change a predicted outcome in a flash. However, you can use muscle testing to help you determine whether certain actions or steps will be strong or weak for you or your business. For other possible uses, I recommend that you explore Dr. Hawkins' book.

What Does Your Body Reveal?

If you're still a bit leery about believing in the intelligence of your body and its ability to reveal your emotions, consider the study of body language. Experts in this field can tell you when someone is lying, when they're confident, when they feel threatened, or if they're likely to buy the product you're selling.

While most people enjoy reading articles in the paper about expert analysis on the body language of politicians, the underlying premise of body language is profound. According to Allan and Barbara Pease, the authors of *The Definitive Book of Body Language*, "Body language is an outward reflection of a person's emotional condition. Each gesture or movement can be a valuable key to an emotion a person may be feeling at the time."[37]

Whether or not you're consciously aware of it, you're using the other person's body language to generate an impression of them and to determine whether or not to do business with them. Research conducted by the Peases suggests that "body language accounts for between 60 and 80 percent of the impact made around a negotiating table."[38]

Just as muscle testing shows, your body is aware of and can't help but express how you feel about something. And how you feel about something or someone, as we learned in the previous chapter, is guidance from your soul or Highest Self about what serves you and what isn't in your best interest.

My Gut Told Me It Was a Bad Idea

While General Manager of a division of Sierra On-Line, I was involved with an acquisition eagerly sought after by the leaders of one of our product lines and supported by upper management. The acquisition never felt right to me, and I didn't want to do it. However, I could never articulate why and didn't have any confidence in my intuition at that point, so I went along with the team who'd be immediately responsible for managing the new group and the rest of the key players in this acquisition.

Nothing went right from the moment we signed the deal; however, I put a lot of effort into trying to make it work. At one point, I flew to New York City for some meetings and ended up meeting with a group of gentlemen from a potential partner (or competitor) in a hotel room.

I felt uncomfortable from the moment I arrived and couldn't wait to escape. I chalked up my upset stomach and uneasiness to being tired, ignorant, and out of my element (the business we acquired was not my area of expertise and these men were all 'experts' in the industry, as it was their sole area of focus). If only I had trusted my gut from the beginning.

Within a matter of weeks, it became clear that these businessmen were trying to find out what I knew about their efforts to acquire an external contractor that was doing critical work for the company we'd recently acquired (now part of my division). They'd seen the contract between Sierra On-Line and the external contractor, felt they could safely back out of the contract once they'd acquired this group, and then use the situation to their advantage. Well, it worked as they'd hoped.

Looking back, I believe my gut knew something was terribly wrong from the beginning. Even though 'it' couldn't articulate what was wrong, it gave me clues from the moment we were looking at the deal. The problem was I didn't have enough confidence in myself or my gut to risk the likely ridicule from sharing what I *felt* with my staff and with upper management. While my body couldn't have predicted all that would happen after the acquisition was made, I believe it 'read' the situation and knew this company and its work was simply not a match strategically or culturally for Sierra On-Line.

What Does Your Little Brain Have to Say?

Check in with your 'little brain,' also known as your enteric nervous system. Turns out your gut has a mind of its own, with neural circuitry or processing capabilities that need little, if any, information from the brain in your head. This little brain makes a slew of decisions about how to process whatever shows up in your gut and communicates with your brain as well. Your gut might receive information from your nonconscious mind before it enters your awareness, so your gut picks up on your anxiety before you do. This connection between the brains is so compelling there is even a field of neurogastroenterology to better understand how the gut affects the brain and vice versa.[39]

Today, if faced with the same set of circumstances, I might still not feel comfortable sharing what my body was telling me, but I'd use my body's knowledge to find the data, the argument, or the proof to offer a more left-brain, logical reason for my concerns. I'd trust my little brain.

The next time your body offers you information, pay attention and incorporate its wisdom in a way that is acceptable to you and anyone else involved.

Take Your Body's Advice

In a tele-class on how to use the power of visualization to achieve the success you desire, I offered ideas to help Anita create a compelling vision for a promotion to a newly created position in her company. Over the phone, I could hear her taking down notes and felt her concentration.

At one point, I felt inspired to offer a completely different idea about envisioning herself sitting down with her new boss, ninety days after starting her new position. Anita would imagine herself hearing words of praise for the wonderful job she was doing, visually seeing the confirmation that she was off to a fast start. This visualization would not show it, but would obviously convey that she had won the job and she had the skills to excel at the job.

Anita stopped writing, laughed and said, "That's great! It wasn't at all where I thought you were going with your idea, but I love it. I felt chills up and down my spine, and knew—from the workshop on intuition I took with you—that I needed to pay attention when I felt those chills."

Anita was not cold, so there was no physical reason she should have chills running up and down her spine. For her, those chills signaled that she had 'hit' upon the visualization idea that was best for her. In addition to her chills, I could hear the shift in her energy because of the tone of her voice and the excitement she conveyed.

Imagine now that I shared some research that indicated that nine out of ten people achieve success when visualizing their new manager or client (if self-employed) shaking their hand, saying "You've got the job!"

What should Anita do? Honor the research and create that visualization or stick with the visualization idea that gave her chills?

As far as I'm concerned, the correct answer is to obviously go with what 'lights her up.' Or, if she feels they both support her goal, use both. We are all unique. When we see 'conclusive' research, we never consider why it didn't work for one out of ten or whatever the percentage failure rate. We like to think we're wired like those the method, drug, or product worked for. But remember, no two brains are wired exactly the same way.

Trust what your inner guidance is telling you. Data's wonderful for helping you to ask the right questions, explore all of the options, or give you ideas about executing your plan. But data is from past history involving other people, not you. And even if the data is about you, the *you* viewing the data is literally a different person from the person involved in the past experience.

If you don't feel comfortable honoring your inner guidance 100 percent or you're not sure that the signal your body sent was truly an intuitive or aha! experience, then have a second choice that you explore simultaneously until you get a clear signal. Or, in a situation you face, find a way to slowly move down the path your "goosebumps, butterflies in your stomach, or chills up and down your spine" told you to take, while spending time determining the optimal next steps if you heed the data you've received.

Pay attention to whether doors are flying open for you and how you feel about the steps you're taking. If you're on the right path, it will quickly become clear to you. If not, turn to your back-up plan that incorporates the data you received.

Change Your Position, Change Your Emotions!

Research shows that if you change your thoughts, you create a different chemical cocktail, so you change your emotions, and that's reflected in your body. Well, Allen and Barbara Pease tell us the opposite is true as well.

> Because of the phenomenon of cause and effect,
> if you intentionally assume certain body-language
> positions you will begin to experience the emotions
> associated with those gestures.[40]

For example, if you 'force' yourself to smile, you cannot help but lighten up and improve your mood. Or, the steeple gesture (hands, with finger tips touching to make the shape of a church steeple) is a powerful show of confidence, but is not always appropriate or natural-looking in a meeting. However, if you practice this gesture repeatedly before going into an important meeting, you can boost your level of confidence.

While you may not be able to replicate the chills, goosebumps, butterflies in the stomach, warmth in the heart, or other physical signs to pay attention to what you're hearing or what's going on around you,

you can practice feeling the physical confidence of having made the right decision. Where in your body would you expect to feel your confidence in your decision?

What if Dr. Schulz is right? What if your body's aches, pains, and signals are part of your innate intelligence and intuition network? How might you treat your body differently, knowing how essential its wisdom is to safely navigating your way through the twists and turns of life?

....

Inspired Questions, Actions, and Leaps

Start paying attention to where in your body you usually feel certain emotions. For example, when you're angry, where in your body do you typically feel that anger? Is it a tightness in your chest, a knot in your belly, clenched hands, or ???

Practice 'locating' the place in your body where you typically register or feel these emotions:

* Peace

* Joy

* Confidence

* Overwhelm

* Frustration

* Anger

* Fear

* Guilt

* Shame

* Depression

The next time you find yourself with an ache or pain, have a conversation with your body. I know that sounds silly, but consider the possibility that the intelligent energy in the cells affected by the ache or pain might have a message for you. If your 'conversation' could speed up your healing, wouldn't it be worth feeling a little foolish?

A possible source of the ache might pop into your head or a scene from a recent argument might appear in your mind's 'eye.' Take whatever comes to you as a possible clue.

Do a body scan every morning when you wake up and every evening when you're ready to fall asleep. At first you'll probably feel foolish and not 'get' any messages, but if you keep at it, you'll start to sense where your body is out of whack. When you do, envision healing energy permeating every cell of the area and the cells communicating to you the emotional block that *might* have caused the ache. *Remember, this isn't about assuming your thoughts and emotions are the cause of every illness, ache, or pain. It's about paying more attention, so you can 'hear' whatever your body's trying to tell you.*

Practice checking in with your body while in meetings or discussions. Pay attention when you feel a shift in your body. Sometimes it might be because the air conditioning has come on and you're cold, but I'm willing to bet that nine times out of ten, when you notice a shift in your body, it's a message to you to pay attention.

Need An Aha! Moment? Try This!

Walk it out. When doing nothing is not an option for you, or you feel a need to burn some energy in order to allow an aha! moment to happen, take a walk. This can be a very powerful way to get clear on the right next step, particularly at work. Leave your office and go for a twenty-minute walk. Before you leave, take a deep breath and ask your nonconscious mind to solve a particular problem for you and guide you to the correct answer.

As you walk out the door, tell yourself that you'll know the next step when you return and then let it go. This is important. The walk is not for going over and over the pros and cons or challenges of possible solutions. The walk is for burning off stressful energy, and clearing the way for your intuition to speak to you. It can't do that if the chatter in your mind about all of the possible outcomes of a decision is nonstop. Distract yourself with the beauty of nature around you, the architecture of the buildings or other physical images. When you start to think about the problem, tell yourself that the answer is coming and imagine it popping into your head soon.

Chapter Seven **Trust Your Gut;
Trust Your Heart**

Barbara (her real name) had just finished a delightful evening with a new friend in her new city of Nashville. Her young son was sleeping peacefully in his car seat in the back, and she was ready to get home. If she remembered the map correctly, there was a shortcut down this back road, so she decided to give it a try and turned on to it.

After driving for awhile in the pitch black, Barbara was beginning to suspect that she'd made a wrong turn or that the road went nowhere. But, like many of us when we're lost, she thought she'd drive just a bit further to see if anything turned up.

All of a sudden, Barbara had a crystal-clear message pop into her head (it wasn't a voice, just a clear knowing or sense): "This isn't right. Stop the car and turn around." There wasn't anyone around her and the sense of *knowing* was compelling, so she didn't hesitate. Barbara stopped the car. As she went to turn around, she could see as far as her headlights, and at the edge of the light, a scary, body-shaking truth hit her. The road completely dropped off!

If Barbara had ignored the guidance in her head, she and her young son would have plunged over a cliff. Who knows why there were no signs or barriers? Perhaps the city of Nashville was so small then, with only locals venturing to the outskirts of town, that no one felt a barrier was necessary, or maybe Barbara had missed a sign along the way.

Whatever the reason, even twenty-plus years later, the thought of that scene still makes Barbara's heart pound.

How did Barbara know just when to stop the car and turn around? She'd just arrived in Nashville and didn't know the back roads at all and had certainly never been down that road during the day or night. So it wasn't a stored memory or experience—as many experts like to think that's all intuition is.

Her story, like many others I've heard, reflects the mysterious power of the *Spiritual Channel of Knowing*. Despite all of the research going on, especially in the area of quantum physics, we have only some intelligent theories to help us make sense of this source of information. Of course, spiritual leaders around the world would say that we have all the information we need.

I'm not interested in convincing you of anything. All I ask is that you consider the possibilities and what those possibilities might mean to how you lead your life. You may be quite familiar with some of the ideas I'll share here. Simply re-consider them and how they might support the idea that you have an Energetic System of Knowing, and, in particular, a Spiritual Channel as part of that system.

The Collective Unconscious: A Field of Energy

Carl Jung, the late, world-respected Swiss psychiatrist, spoke of the collective unconscious to represent the collective human history of wisdom, beliefs, attitudes, superstitions, and fears of our ancestors, represented by a variety of archetypes. When we're born, Jung surmised that we have access to all of this knowledge and all of the archetypes (the good, the wise, the fearful, and the bad), with each of us 'wearing' or 'tapping into' some archetypes more than others. While Jung likely meant this to represent an internal, nonconscious source of information accessible at birth, it fits beautifully with scientific theory.

In his work on Field Theory, biologist Rupert Sheldrake hypothesized that we exist in a world of morphogenetic fields.[41] For example, when we learn to ride a bicycle, we are tapping into the experience or energy of all of those who have come before us who have ridden a bicycle. Another way to think about this is how easy it is for children to learn to use an iPod or a BlackBerry. Adults fumble and try to read the instructions and master these tools (or at least adults like me), but many children seem 'high-tech ready' when they're born. They're highly intuitive at birth and easily able to tap into all of the experience of everyone who's come before them.

As adults, most of us have trained ourselves to ignore this ability to absorb this kind of intuitive information from these morphogenetic fields. However, as more and more people develop an expertise, it becomes easier for the rest of us to tap into it. For example, when athletes break a significant world record, notice how quickly other athletes usually follow. The hypothesis is that these athletes are tapping into the new morphogenetic field created by the athlete who first broke the record.

Using this idea of morphogenetic fields or the collective unconscious, we can turn to Barbara's story and imagine that all of the people who lived in the area of Barbara's friend knew that the road stopped at a cliff. That body of knowledge was part of a morphogenetic field of the territory.

When Barbara was driving on a silent road late at night, she was likely very receptive to picking up energetic clues. In fact, driving on an open highway is considered a great way to tap into your intuition, as your left brain is busy managing the tasks of driving, so your right brain can 'roam' and offer up ideas galore. I know a woman who schedules a yearly road trip for the purpose of brainstorming and tapping into her intuitive wisdom.

In any case, Barbara was likely in a mental space where she could quickly register and heed the collective wisdom of the local people. As far as I know, there is no scientific reason why that is *not* possible. Again, thoughts are bits of energy that do not die. When we are *open* to receiving information, we can pick up on the thoughts around us.

What Color Is Your Aura (or Energy Field)?

I remember rolling my eyes in the 70s and 80s when I heard people talking about auras and what the different colors of auras said about your mental, emotional, and physical state (I grew up in southern California). Oops! Turns out we do have an energy field, or aura, that extends beyond our bodies. It's literally a part of us and is one of the reasons why we have a need for 'space' between ourselves and strangers. We subconsciously don't want to mix our energy field with someone else's. This is also why you can walk into a room, meet someone, and pick up their 'energy.'

So who are you then? Are you your brain? Are you your body? Are you a field of energy? Are you some 'thing' that still exists after your body dies? And, who is driving this thing we call a body anyway?

If this 'it' that we are—this consciousness—is more like a field of energy than a chunk of matter, then doesn't it make sense that we would be capable of drawing into our awareness—our field of energy— the data, information, or wisdom that we need in any given moment? Because isn't that information simply a packet of energy with a certain vibration?

Or do you think (like some scientists) that this thing called consciousness is all in our head—literally a creation of our brain? If you do, or if you simply have some doubts, consider this:

Research conducted by Rollin McCraty, Ph.D. and Mike Atkinson of the HeartMath Research Center and Raymond Trevor Bradley, Ph.D. of the Institute for Whole Social Science supports the idea that the body can register and respond to information *before* we actually experience or see it.[42] While I'm thrilled that scientists are doing carefully (scientifically) tested research that verifies our ability to tap into knowledge outside our conscious awareness, what really struck me when I read the findings of their studies was that their careful analysis of *how* the body registered awareness of the information indicated that the heart—not the brain—was the first to receive and register awareness of the incoming information.

> What is truly surprising about this result is the fact that the heart appears to play a direct role in the perception of future events; at the very least it implies that the brain does not act alone in this regard.

At the end of the summary of their research, the authors offered an acknowledgement that perhaps we're smarter than we think we are and we've known this intuitively all along:

> In closing, although our finding that the heart is involved in intuitive perception may be surprising from one perspective, it is worth noting that in virtually all human cultures, ancient and modern, the heart has long been regarded as a conduit to a source of information and wisdom beyond normal awareness. Thus, our data may be seen as providing scientific evidence for an intuitive capacity that humankind has known and used for many millennia.[43]

What does your heart and intuition say about what the Spiritual Channel of Knowing is and where its wisdom comes from?

An Olympic Aha!

Kelly and her husband were enjoying the 1996 Summer Olympics in Atlanta, Georgia on July 26 and had just finished attending an exciting track and field program. As they tried to board packed subways with thousands of other fans, they realized they could either wait for at least an hour to head back to their hotel, or go in a different direction, to Centennial Olympic Park. They hadn't been to the 'town square' of the Olympic Village, as it was called, where all of the celebration and 'action' apparently was, so they decided to head in that direction.

After spending an hour or two enjoying the live music and people-watching, and capturing it all on video, Kelly's husband suggested checking out the subway crowds. If not too crowded, they could head back to their hotel. If still packed, they'd hang out at Centennial Olympic Park for awhile longer. When they got to the subway station, it was approaching midnight and the subway had only light traffic. Her husband looked at Kelly to see if she still wanted to stay and celebrate, or if she was ready to head back to the hotel. After a moment's hesitation, Kelly had a strong feeling that they *must* go back to the hotel, and said to her husband, "I don't know why, but we're not going back to Centennial Olympic Park."

As Kelly shared this story with me twelve years later, she repeatedly mentioned that fearlessly trusting her gut was unlike her. She's a perfectionist who likes to be sure of herself before making a definitive statement. But she felt compelled to blurt out her firm decision to her husband.

Back at the hotel, Kelly and her husband were shocked to find out that less than an hour after their leaving Centennial Olympic Park, a bomb had exploded right in the area where they'd been 'hanging out.' When Kelly watched the videotape of the scene and her own videotape, she had added confirmation that they'd both been exactly where the bomb exploded. Yes, security guards had been alerted before the bomb exploded and had begun clearing the area, but who knows what would have happened if they had stayed there.

Kelly's aha! moment was clearly not from a bunch of stored memories, but much more like foreknowledge of an event. While she didn't have access to a psychic vision telling her exactly what would happen, she did have access to some form of knowing about what had been planned. Yes, the upcoming bomb explosion was in the future, but the bomb had likely already been planted. Perhaps Kelly accessed wisdom or intelligence from a spiritual source or picked up on the thought or emotional energy of the bomber. We'll never know for certain. But what we can know is that we should pay attention when a strong feeling of knowing comes to us. Better to be safe and feel foolish, than to talk yourself out of what you *feel* is right simply because you can't logically explain it.

Can a Random Event Become Less Random?

The truth is that more and more research confirms we can pick up on changes in the energy fields around us and we can influence those fields as well, especially as a united group of individuals. There are fascinating reports of findings from scientists using highly sophisticated random number or event generators (REGs). Using these sophisticated machines that spit out a random series of 1s and 0s, scientists have found that major disasters, in particular, affect the REGs. They become noticeably less random.

In her book, *The Intention Experiment*, Lynne McTaggart shares the story of the findings of this research. And, in part, the results of these studies compelled her to co-create the worldwide intention experiment (www.theintentionexperiment.com). What's even more bizarre than the idea that as a collective group experiencing a tragedy we can affect the energy and output of a machine is the startling finding that, like Kelly in her Olympic experience, the machines seemed to reflect a premonition of disaster.

> Although activity of the REGs was normal in
> the days leading up to 9/11, the machines became
> increasingly correlated a few hours *before* the first tower
> was hit, as though there had been a mass premonition.
> This similarity in output continued for two days after
> the first strike.[44]

If that doesn't make you pause and wonder how this world we live in is wired, I don't know what would. The research had begun years before the 9/11 catastrophe and led to the creation of The Global Consciousness Project (GCP) in 1998, run by director Roger Nelson at Princeton University (noosphere.princeton.edu). As stated on their website, the Project's purpose is to "examine subtle correlations that reflect the presence and activity of consciousness in the world. We have learned that when millions of us share intentions and emotions the GCP/EGG network shows correlations."[45]

The mind-blowing work of the Global Consciousness Project dovetails beautifully with the work of The Institute of HeartMath and the nonprofit organization they created, The Global Coherence Project (www.globalcoherenceproject.org). After years of studying the heart, its intelligence, and its role in communicating with the brain and the rest of the body, these experts on the heart have reviewed the leading-edge work of The Global Consciousness Project and are now collaborating with Dr. Elizabeth Rauscher, Ph.D., astrophysicist and nuclear scientist, and other top scientists to create a Global Coherence Monitoring System (GCMS). This system will "directly measure fluctuations in the magnetic fields generated by the earth and in the ionosphere." (The ionosphere is the outer segment or edge of the earth's atmosphere.)

As mentioned in Chapter Six, but worth noting again, The Institute of HeartMath has found a direct link or communication between the coherence of the heart's rhythm and the emotions we're feeling at any given time. When we experience positive emotions, our heart's beating pattern is "smooth, ordered, coherent" and that message is relayed via the heart's magnetic field (approximately five thousand times more powerful than the brain's magnetic field) to the rest of the body. When we experience negative emotions, our heart's beating pattern is "erratic, disordered, incoherent."

When you combine the work of The Institute of HeartMath with the work of The Global Consciousness Project, the next step is to see if consciously creating more coherent heartbeat patterns on a global level can positively impact the magnetic field of the earth. While this may seem preposterous, the more we learn about how energy links us all together, the less strange this seems. To find out more about their work, visit www.globalcoherenceproject.org.

The World Wide Web of Energy— of Connection

The idea that we're all connected via an intricate web of energy fields and can therefore access a wide range of intelligence on an energetic level and therefore influence—and be influenced by—the world around us sounds suspiciously like we create our own reality. And it suggests that talk of one world, one universal intelligence, one cosmic or God consciousness isn't weird or 'woo-woo' at all. It's only when we insist upon staying in our heads, determined to use only tangible data or expert opinion, that we shut down our ability to access this intelligence and enjoy the connection.

Perhaps the very American image of the self-sufficient and independent man or woman fighting to be free to do things his or her way has caused many of us to be fearful of the idea of being connected to one another and being able to read each other's energy. We jump to the conclusion that it means giving up our freedom or having someone's thoughts and ideas invade our space in an attempt to control us.

Just as there are always risks with a team effort versus an individual effort, when the team is united and bringing out the best of all, the team can accomplish so much more than an individual can. In the same way, imagine the quality of your decisions and the brilliance of your ideas when you're able to tap into the wisdom of cosmic consciousness. And, finally, consider how alone we can all feel when we're embarking upon a new venture. How wonderful it would be to be reminded of the connection we have with one another and with those who have gone before us.

Our Profound Connection—One Astronaut's Experience

Have you ever had an experience where you felt that connection? One of the most documented experiences of this—and perhaps most respected—was the former astronaut Edgar Mitchell's epiphany on his return to Earth while part of the Apollo 14 space mission. Mitchell's epiphany was so strong that he felt compelled to band with like-minded, traditionally educated and trained scientists to begin to explore inner space with the same rigorous methods used in testing hypotheses in those more traditional areas of science. With his friends' help, Mitchell founded the Institute of Noetic Sciences (IONS), a nonprofit organization dedicated to "exploring the frontiers of consciousness."

I urge you to check out the IONS website (www.noetic.org). There you'll find Mitchell's powerful story of his life-changing epiphany and other information to stretch your thinking. Here's a small excerpt of Mitchell's experience from the website:

> Sitting in the cramped cabin of the space capsule, he saw planet Earth floating freely in the vastness of space. He was engulfed by a profound sense of universal connectedness—an epiphany. In Mitchell's own words: "The presence of divinity became almost palpable, and I knew that life in the universe was not just an accident based on random processes.... The knowledge came to me directly."
>
> Mitchell faced a critical challenge. As a physical scientist, he had grown accustomed to directing his attention to the objective world "out there." But the experience that came to him in space led him to a startling hypothesis: Perhaps reality is more complex, subtle, and inexorably mysterious than conventional science had led him to believe. Perhaps a deeper understanding of consciousness (inner space) could lead to a new and expanded view of reality in which objective and subjective, outer and inner, are understood as co-equal aspects of the miracle and mystery of being.[46]

The Energy of Universal Love—My Moment of Connection

For a few moments, I too felt deep within me that 'sense of universal connectedness,' or the awe of the love that can permeate every cell of your being. I was attending Peak Potential's Enlightened Wizard Camp, which was a powerful and life-changing experience.

On the last night of the camp, I was involved in an 'exercise' or 'process' with the more than two-hundred-fifty other participants.

When we all walked into the main hall that night, we had no idea what to expect. Since I agreed to go first, my partner for the exercise, JoAnn, would support me through the process and make sure I was okay. She'd get any assistance from the trained staff if necessary.

After completing the process, we had a short break to allow those of us who went first to relax, and then it was time to switch places. Next, I got to support JoAnn. While most of the room was in semi-darkness, with people lying down on the carpet on blankets with their designated partner next to them, JoAnn and I were under the one set of overhead lights left on. At the time, I was a bit peeved about this, as I didn't necessarily want a spotlight on me. Well, the light overhead turned out to be a gift, as it enabled me to really look around the room at one point when JoAnn was resting with her eyes closed. My eyes picked up all of these people (who—in many cases—hadn't known each other before the start of the camp and likely wouldn't see each other again) who were comforting, and sometimes holding with care and compassion, their partner as he or she was releasing or processing past emotions and memories.

I was already starting to feel this deep sense of love emanating from my heart when my eyes landed on two men who were part of my team. Based on what I had witnessed throughout the week, I would describe both of them as mentally and physically fit leaders. The man going through the 'process' was sitting up and clearly dealing with some emotional memories. Dave, as I'll call him (not his real name), was trained in the military and had a great sense of humor, but thought some of the concepts covered during the week a bit 'out there.' I'd describe him as being closer to the stereotypical macho male. Joe (also not his real name), although you could tell he was a gentler soul, also had a strong presence within our team, leading the way in a number of challenging exercises.

The presence of divinity became almost palpable, and I knew that life in the universe was not just an accident based on random processes.... The knowledge came to me directly.

Edgar Mitchell, Ph.D.

As my eyes landed on the two of them, Dave was sitting up, hunched over, being comforted with such care and compassion by Joe that it brought tears to my eyes. It still does. My eyes are welling up as I write these words. In that moment, I felt this deep connection with everyone in the room and with everyone on the planet. Witnessing those two men who'd never met before that week participating fully, with open hearts, opened my heart as well and enabled me to see how we are all connected.

Now, like Edgar Mitchell and others, I *know* I am connected to everything on this planet, especially every human being, and I know that my consciousness is part of a divine consciousness. I may not experience it the same way others do, or wrap it in the religious wrapping many do, but I know—like the heart knows—that my Spiritual Channel of Knowing is open (except in moments of fear) and able to receive all of the wisdom and guidance I will ever need. All I need to do is stay connected.

Perhaps you've had a similar experience, or know of someone else who did. Perhaps you think it's a bunch of hooey. Whatever your perspective, all I ask is that you consider the possibilities of what a Spiritual Channel of Knowing and global energetic connection might mean for your big life choices and for even those small decisions that you need to make every day. What if you could draw on the wisdom of the wisest soul you know of every time you have to make a decision? What if you could connect energetically with others in times of depression or sorrow—no matter where you are—to pull you out? What could you accomplish then?

Inspired Questions, Actions, and Leaps

✳ Do you consider yourself a spiritual person? What does being 'spiritual' mean to you?

✳ How do you know you've experienced a spiritual connection or a spiritual moment?

✳ Take your personal experiences and define what a Spiritual Channel of Knowing would look like to you. For example, could this channel be your 'hotline' to God, Jesus, Buddha, Mohammad, Moses, Source Energy, Father/Mother Spirit, or beloved ancestors? Or does it make more sense to you to envision it as an intricate web of connections to everyone? (Everyone alive? Everyone who's ever lived? Everyone who lived, is living now, and who will live?)

✳ If you don't consider yourself very spiritual, if at all, could the idea of 'testing' potential decisions against your values and your professional and personal mission or vision work for you? If so, take some time to get clear on what your most cherished values are and what the key components of your mission are. You'll need to be able to access these quickly in order to 'test' ideas and decisions against them.

✳ Have you ever had a 'profound sense of universal connectedness' like Edgar Mitchell? If so, have you written it down or recorded the experience? Think about how powerfully that memory would bring your heartbeat pattern into coherence.

Need An Aha! Moment? Try This!

Look Through Another's Eyes. A few years ago the question some Christians were recommended to ask themselves before making a decision was "What Would Jesus Do?" (WWJD). Whatever your spiritual beliefs, the idea of momentarily stepping into someone else's shoes is a great way to loosen the hold of your past experiences, beliefs, or thought patterns. Come up with a list of divine beings, spiritual leaders, business or world leaders, and family and friends you admire. Imagine them as your own personal board of directors for your life. When you have a decision to make, go through your list. Who on that list would be best to check in with for their point of view on the current situation you're facing?

Set aside a few moments to close your eyes and imagine this person or divine presence is with you right now. What would they have to say about your decision? Note whatever ideas or images come to you and pay attention to how simply shifting your perspective can bring clarity to a challenging decision.

Aha!

Chapter Eight Check In With
Your Energetic System of Knowing

Sara stared at the array of packages in front of her. She was in way over her head, and she knew it. But she was determined to get her unique women's hosiery product launched. How hard could it be? Really hard. As she stared at her new package design, Sara turned her gaze to compare it to the competitors' packages. Did her package have all of the same legal stuff they did? Sara didn't have a budget for a lot of attorney's fees, so she used her head and trusted her gut to help her make a lot of her decisions.

But this was a really big decision. "Is this package final? Should I begin production?" Sara wondered. She got up from her desk, walked over to the window, closed her eyes for a moment, and checked in with her gut. She had her answer. She came back to her desk and told her team her decision.

This was just one of the intuitive decision moments that led to the launch of Spanx, a $150 million+ in revenue women's hosiery business. Sara Blakely's initial aha! moment came when she was determined to find an undergarment. In frustration at not finding what she needed, she cut off the feet of pantyhose and wore those. After trying to find an existing manufacturer to make what she was sure many other women would want, she decided to do it herself. Despite knowing nothing about either running a business or the hosiery industry and having countless doors slammed in her face, Sara persisted and found one supplier who would work with her.

Sara's story is posted in more detail on the Spanx website (including how she came up with the name). In person, Sara describes making most of her decisions just like she made the package decision, even after having employees around her. When a decision needed to be made, Sara would go into a quiet corner, close her eyes, and check in with her gut. Her gut never steered her wrong.

In the midst of the successful growth of her business and with a strong CEO in place, Sara followed her gut and heart again—despite opposition—and took time off to participate in the 2004 Fox TV reality show: *The Rebel Billionaire: Richard Branson's Quest for the Best.*

Out of that 'trust your gut' decision came a first runner-up finish in the contest, a wealth of life-changing experiences, and a surprise check for $750,000 (Branson gave her his paycheck from Fox), so Sara could start her own foundation to help other less fortunate women honor and bring to life their own aha! moments. When Sara felt compelled to join the TV show, perhaps her gut could sense all the possibilities that exposure to Richard Branson and the other participants could give her. Sara's logical mind and outside, well-meaning friends and experts who tried to tell her it was a distraction didn't have the bigger picture in mind.

Look Within for Your Answer

Sara had to look within for many of her answers because she didn't have external resources available to her. When we have the time and money to do all of the research and check in with all of the experts, we can lose sight of the power of our own inner guidance system. It can guide us to the right package design just as easily as to the right relationship. All we need to do is begin using it on a regular basis. Like Sara, try acting as if you don't have the external resources available to you when it comes time to make a decision. Go within and tap into the wealth of wisdom available to you via your Energetic System of Knowing.

Use the data and expert opinion to form clear questions, options, timing of actions, or possible next steps. Then step away from facts that are nothing more than *past* behavior or results that have very little, if anything, to do with *now*. No one is the same as they were a moment ago, let alone as they were when they made a recommendation a year ago.

Make Wise Decisions: Use Your Wise Mind

Wise decisions come from a blend or integration of judgment, discernment, and comprehension. With your wise mind, make a *judgment* about what the real question that you're asking is or what answer you're looking for. Then, *discern* how you feel—physically and emotionally—about the answer or idea that comes to you, and finally, take time to *comprehend* fully—mentally, emotionally, physically, and spiritually—what is right for you at any given moment.

Once your final decision has been made, go back to judgment (left brain) to outline the possible next steps and action plans and repeat the cycle.

Wise Mind Discernment
and Action Process

What's the Optimal Answer, Choice, or Right Next Step?

1. Use Your Head

a. Get clear in your head (left brain) what it is you're asking your whole mind (mental, emotional, physical, and spiritual ways of knowing) to work on. What's the true question or challenge you need help with?

b. If at all possible, write down the question. This solidifies it in your mind and puts more energy into the question. You're telling your nonconscious mind that you're serious and willing to pay attention for the answer.

2. Listen to Your Heart

a. Pay attention! Your 'heart' (physical heart, as well as your right brain) won't send you an e-mail with 'answer to your question' in the subject heading. So if you're running around all day frantically multi-tasking, you'll never hear, feel, or sense the answer when it comes.

b. Get quiet. Even if only for a minute, close your eyes, take a deep breath, and imagine the answer you need winging its way to you or being pulled out of the vast storage space of all the memories your nonconscious mind has access to.

c. Be on the look-out for thoughts 'popping' into your head, images triggering ideas or answers, lyrics from a song on the radio inspiring you, or the right book showing up and you intuitively opening it to the right page.

3. Trust Your Gut

a. When you have a 'sense' that the answer has come, check in with your gut or intuitive network. Do you feel the rightness of the answer in your body? Where? In your gut?

In your chest? Up and down your spine? With goosebumps?

b. How does the answer or idea sit with you emotionally? Does it feel positive? Do you have a sense of peace and calm with the answer? Pay attention to how peace feels to you. Intuitive answers don't always generate strong positive emotion like wishful thinking does. They just feel right. The sense of peace and clarity that comes to you tells you that you've hit upon the right answer.

Given My Answer, What Inspired Action Should I Now Take?

4. Use Your Head

a. Now that you have the insight you need, what's the right next step for you? For example, if you've been struggling with finding something that makes your heart sing and you finally receive the answer that you've been searching for— say, volunteer work with the elderly—you need to figure out what to do next.

b. Use your head to quickly list all of the possible ways to proceed that come to mind, to get an idea of how much time you'd like to devote to this activity and to establish a target date for when you'd like to start.

c. But don't make any decisions just yet. Now check in with your heart.

5. Listen to Your Heart

a. Sit with your tentative ideas and decisions for a moment. Ask yourself, "Are there any ideas or possible next steps I'm missing?"

b. Also ask yourself, "Does the timing and time commitment *feel* right to me? Am I excited? Do I feel as if I'm taking on too much if I commit that much time? Can I create a picture in my mind of me doing this work in a way that lights me up?"

6. Trust Your Gut

a. You know the drill by now. Check in with your Energetic System of Knowing for each and every piece of the puzzle. Yes, I do mean every piece. While this may seem awkward initially, you'll quickly be able to do this in a matter of minutes or even seconds.

b. By taking the time to check in, you send a powerful message to every cell of your being that you're open to all of the wisdom and guidance available to you at any given moment. As you develop trust in this process and practice it regularly, it will help you in moments of panic and confusion. You've got the process down. You breathe and you run through it. Then, even in a hectic work environment, the clarity that you need comes.

Like Sara Blakely, many entrepreneurs go through this process consciously or unconsciously without realizing this is exactly what they're doing. Entrepreneurs develop this ability because they have to. They rarely have access to the data or expertise (or dollars to generate it) that people in the corporate world do. However, no matter what the setting or situation may be, you can take yourself and your team through this process before making a decision.

Depending upon how open others are to integrating intuition with reason, you can always use this process on your own and then let it guide you to the data you need to convince others. If someone's not open to intuition, even when blended with reason, there's no point in trying to convince them of the power of this approach. Just use it on your own and trust that the same intelligence that guides you to the optimal answer will guide you to the practical, tangible information you might need to build your case.

Pull Out Your Sword and Cut Through the Clutter

At times you'll find yourself overwhelmed by the options, the confusing and conflicting data and opinions of others, and the incessant chatter of your own inner critic. You know you need an aha! moment. Sometimes a powerful symbol or visualization can bring clarity to a cluttered mind.

An aha! moment is "the mind that has no doubt," as cultural anthropologist Angeles Arrien, Ph.D. describes it in *The Tarot Handbook*. In her book, Arrien provides a rich symbolic, cultural, and psychological review of the meaning of the imagery of each of the tarot cards of the Thoth Deck, one of the most respected tarot card decks available. In her analysis of the Ace of Swords tarot card, Arrien explains that it symbolizes the aha! experience or "the mind that has no doubt."[47]

A Note On Using the Tarot

Some people feel very uncomfortable with the idea of using tarot or other card decks. If it's not for you, that's okay. I've personally found them to be invaluable in regaining my own intuitive abilities, connecting with my faith, and bringing me into my wise mind. The key is to be playful about it and to always check in with your inner guidance and not rely solely on what the card 'says.'

If you're like me, when you've got an important problem or challenge to deal with, your mind typically gets caught up in the notion that it must think its way through to a solution. So it bounces back and forth between options, opinions, facts, figures, and emotional reactions to each of the options. Because the mind is running in an endless loop of possibilities, worries, fears, and doubts, the idea of quieting down the internal mental chatter and experiencing a "mind that has no doubt" is immediately appealing and a powerful way to think about aha! moments.

Your Sword of Insight

The Ace of Swords is also associated with the story of King Arthur pulling the sword out of the stone, which led to his being crowned king. It represents that powerful sword. Imagine such a sword at your disposal to cut through all of the choices, fears, and data to arrive at the ideal answer and to the mental state of a mind that has no doubt. For example, using the sword as an image for the aha! experience, imagine that you now hold a *sword of insight*. Whether you see yourself as a Japanese Samurai warrior, a knight of the Round Table, or Xena: Warrior Princess, imagine that this mighty sword is imbued with energy from all four ways of knowing: mental, emotional, physical, and spiritual. Now lift it high and imagine wielding it to pierce through all of the confusion, doubts, fears, and overload of information that can clutter your mind when you're faced with major decisions. Visualize this *sword of insight* piercing through to the ideal solution, insight, or bright idea that you desire.

Like Arthur as a boy, we all have the potential to simply grasp the sword and effectively use it to get the clarity and guidance we seek. However, as adults who spend too much time focused on thinking, most of us are like the hardened knights of the King Arthur tale; we've forgotten how to claim and use, on a regular basis, this seemingly elusive power, the power of the aha! moment.

Play: The Real Secret to Success

I know it doesn't make sense, but treating your big life decisions (and even small ones) playfully gives you the best chance to intuit what the right decision is for you. When you are stressed out, anxious to solve a problem, or determined to take immediate action to correct something in your life, you are turning or closing off all of your internal receptor sites or channels. What does energy do? It flows. What happens when it gets blocked? It consolidates and explodes to release the built-up pressure. And, that explosion usually results in words or behavior you soon regret.

When you take a break to play, you breathe life and energy into constricted cells and you allow all of the universal intelligence available to you to flow in. Sometimes all you need is a brief distraction to allow a memory to bubble up from your nonconscious mind and sometimes you need a long walk, a few games of solitaire, or a fierce table tennis match. We've all had the experience of being distracted by someone or something, only to realize that in that moment of distraction, the answer or idea we needed popped into our head. An understanding of this is leading more companies to encourage play breaks for their employees.

However, many of us are guilty of feeling guilty (a double dose of guilt!) about taking time to play. As a recovering workaholic, I can certainly be counted in that group. My first true understanding and knowing of the power of play came after I'd launched Inspired Leap. I would put that experience right up there with other life-changing aha! moments I've had.

My Playful Aha! Moment

In the spring of 2003, I was excited to be speaking at my first conference as the founder of Inspired Leap Consulting. Integrity was a real hot button, as corporate scandals seemed to be showing up daily in the news. My topic blended the concept of integrity with accessing intuition. A recovering corporate burn-out 'victim' (self-inflicted), I confess I had an aversion to PowerPoint. No offense to Microsoft, but if I never had to sit through another PowerPoint presentation, I'd be happy. However, I always honor the preferred presentation style of clients, and, in this case, they wanted a PowerPoint presentation. The client also wanted the *slides* thirty days before the conference, so printed copies could be made available to participants as handouts.

In my zeal to prepare my presentation, I misunderstood what was needed by the Friday deadline. Late Thursday afternoon, I was thrilled to have a detailed handout and an outline of my presentation—but no PowerPoint. I knew I had a month left to get the PowerPoint presentation prepared for my breakout session, so I was relaxed and feeling quite proud of myself. That afternoon, I found out that my handout was fine, but what they really needed by the next day was the complete PowerPoint presentation. I almost came unglued.

After carefully hanging up the phone, I took a deep breath but could feel the emotions of anger and fear, not to mention a big pity party, coming on. I took another deep breath and got up, left the computer, and went downstairs to play with my dog for about an hour. I fixed a quick bite to eat, then went back upstairs to my office refreshed. I immediately noticed the clarity of my thinking and how easily I was able to get into the flow of transforming my Word document into a PowerPoint presentation. I delivered the completed presentation early the next afternoon—by deadline.

I know this may be a silly example for some of you. For me, however, it was a major shift and a break in a bad pattern of behavior. All of the times when I'd been a martyr to a deadline (real or self-imposed), a last-minute change in plans, or a new idea from a boss and pushed myself to keep working when I was really past the point of being productive, I'd done myself and my company a huge disservice. By not being deliberate about taking a break to play, I wasn't allowing in all of the intelligence and thinking ability at my disposal. And, therefore, I took even longer to get things done and created a vicious cycle of more work, less play, and therefore more work and a bad attitude that got worse with each repetition of the cycle.

While I'm not perfect at remembering to take a play break, I've never been the same since. Something shifted within me, and I'll never talk myself out of a play break again. When I feel I need one, I take one. And I'm still delighted every time I come back to work to find that my creative ideas and productivity soar. The pleasure of that mental reward (a clear mind) after doing something frivolous never gets old.

What's in Your Bag of Tricks?

Imagine that you've just received word that the presentation to senior management you've been painstakingly preparing is going to be moved up to tomorrow morning instead of two weeks from today. It's now three o'clock, and it's already been an exhausting day. What do you do? How do you handle it?

If you can't see yourself in this situation, come up with another scenario that would be realistic for you. In those moments, it's easy to slip into the "Oh darn" (I'd say something a bit stronger) mode and run around in a panic. So, it's important to have a plan *before* the situation ever comes up. First, create a list of a variety of playful, relaxing activities you can do for anywhere from fifteen minutes to an hour. For example, my list would include:

1. Play solitaire on the computer

2. Take a walk around the block

3. Play ball with Forest (my dog)

4. Put on some high-energy music and stretch or dance

5. Call a friend (one who I know will be positive)

6. Color – I've developed a love for coloring mandalas (bringing back into my life a childhood pleasure with a spiritual twist)

Research suggests that the best activities on my list are likely to be the walk, playing with Forest, or moving to music. Why? Well, it turns out that the brain's performance noticeably improves after exercise or movement, as any athlete or person dedicated to fitness will tell you. Because of this, try to have at least one movement activity on your list.

Now come up with five-minute, fifteen-minute, thirty-minute, and sixty-minute versions of them. You no longer have a reason to ignore the inner call to take a break and play. Everyone, including you, can find five to fifteen minutes in her day for a play break.

A Quiet Corner

Spanx founder Sara Blakely would stand up and walk to a corner or window to check in with her gut before making a big decision. We all need a 'quiet corner,' even if it's only in our heads. What kind of process would work best for you? Can you dedicate a corner of your home or office for checking in with your gut or Energetic System of Knowing? Put something that reminds you of quiet, reflection, and receiving inner guidance in that space. No one else needs to know the special meaning of the item; it's just a symbol for you. Your intuitive right brain loves symbols and images, so include them in your space.

If finding a physical place to check in makes you feel uncomfortable or isn't realistic, create a place in your head. Use your power of visualization to imagine a place where every time you imagine yourself there, you calm down and connect with your inner guidance. You can train yourself to relax and be open to answers by repeating the visualization whenever you need help. Make it a room or a wide-open space in nature. It doesn't matter, as long as you get the meditative feeling and focus you need to access your inner guidance.

Go On an Inner Journey

Take yourself on a guided visualization when you find it difficult to focus. You may already have a few to choose from. If not, consider my audio CD, *Envision Your Way to Success*, which contains four guided visualizations, along with inspiring stories and information to rev up your imagination. Or, check out the classic *Creative Visualization* book or audio CD, by Shakti Gawain.

For now, read the visualization below, then close your eyes and take yourself to the space described. Or create an audio CD of your own voice reading this visualization, or download an audio version of this at www.TheAhaMomentsBook.com/visualization.

Find the Answer You Seek: Take Yourself on an Inner Journey

Remember the movie *Mary Poppins*? There was a scene with Mary and the children looking at Bert's lovely chalk drawings on the pavement. And then they jumped into one of them. During this meditation, you'll be asked to go through the same process. At one point, you'll be witnessing yourself in a scene and then I'll ask you to jump right in to become a part of it.

So let's begin...

We're going to start by getting centered and calm. First, shake out your legs, arms, and body. Imagine shaking off any tension you may have been feeling. Now sit down in a comfortable chair (you can lie down only if you trust you won't fall asleep!). Take a deep, deep belly breath. Imagine breathing in all the way down to your toes. Now hold that breath a moment, then slowly release it, imagining that you are emptying your body of all old, negative thoughts and feelings. Do this one more time.

Now close your eyes and know that you are safe.

Imagine that you're staying at a private, luxurious lakeside cabin. Your deck looks directly onto a large, deep, blue-green lake where the only movement comes from the ducks lazily moving across from one shore to the other. They're obviously not in a hurry and neither are you.

You're dressed perfectly for this sunny spring day, so you take your cup of coffee, tea, or another preferred beverage and head out to the most comfortable deck chair you've ever sat in. As you gaze out to the glassy surface of the lake and sip your drink, you begin to recall something you want to create in your life. It may be something completely different than you expected, but on this gorgeous morning you're willing to dream about and 'play' with any scene or idea.

You set down your cup and actively call up the images, sounds, feelings, and smells of that very special dream. Immerse yourself into the vision or dream for a moment. You no longer notice the lake, the deck chair, or your drink.

After what seems like a few moments, you hear the call of a bird and glance up. The glassy lake seems to beckon you, so you get up, stretch, and head down a short dirt path to a private dock where a rowboat and canoe are. You don't pay too much attention to them, but move on to the edge of the dock and look down.

The smooth, blue-green surface of the lake is a perfect mirror this morning. You gaze into this mirror and see your beautiful self. That's right. You really SEE who you truly are—you glimpse your inner beauty.

As you continue to gaze into the lake—your special

mirror this morning—you notice that a vibrant scene is unfolding in this mirror before your eyes. There you are in the scene you just imagined. Who's there with you? Anyone? What are the sounds, images, scents, and other items in this scene? You realize that this is a mental rehearsal of what is to come. And then you feel yourself mentally 'jump' into the scene.

Now you truly FEEL the active experience of having what you want come to be. What's it like? How do you feel? Can you even describe it? ENJOY this experience for a moment. Know that time is no barrier right now. You are TRULY there, participating in the scene.

After a few moments of your enjoying this experience, the water begins to ripple from a few beautiful, vibrant blue, green, and black ducks swimming by. You slowly turn around and walk back up to the deck, with the only sounds an occasional call of a bird and the lapping of the water along the shore.

As you walk up the steps to the deck, you ask yourself, "What's the right next step for me to bring this wonderful scene into reality?"

Now imagine that your question is being sent to every cell of your being and out into the universe. Your only job is to wait comfortably, trusting that the answer to your question is coming.

You peacefully move towards that wonderful deck chair and notice that there's an envelope sitting in the chair. You reach down and pick it up. It's addressed to you and at the bottom there's a note that says: *Your answer is inside.* It may be an image, a written answer, a scent, a voice, or piece of music. Trust that what you find when you open the envelope is just what you're meant to find. You open up the envelope and find your answer.

Take a moment to absorb all that you need from

your answer. If there was nothing there, trust that the work is still being done and the answer will come.

Thank whoever you think provided you with the answer and the visualization that you needed.

You sit back down and feel great sitting in the deck chair—the stress is gone. You know that whether or not you received a clear answer, the next step will come to you soon and you've paved the way for your scene— your dream to come to you.

You take another sip of your drink, then stretch your arms to the sky to express your joy in the moment. When you're ready, open your eyes. To download an audio version of this guided visualization, go to www.TheAhaMomentsBook.com/visualization.

Use your imagination to create your own guided visualizations to help you access your inner guidance whenever you need it.

As you learn more about your Energetic System of Knowing and how those intuitive channels best 'speak' to you, you'll find the activities that work best for you. We're all different. What works best for one person is boring or uncomfortable for another. Trust yourself. The important thing is to find activities that you can deliberately, with focused intent, use to check in with all four channels of knowing.

Some people (maybe you're one of them) enjoy meditating and relish the time to sit quietly. Others, like me, do meditate, but find quieting my mind more difficult while sitting still than while coloring, drawing, or even playing solitaire. Pick what works for you and stick with it. Just as with creating your own inner place for accessing your inner guidance, you'll train yourself to quickly get quiet and go within whenever you begin your chosen activity.

There is a wealth of intelligence at your disposal. The catch is that you have to slow down enough to see, hear, or feel it, as it flows through and around you. Are you listening?

....
Inspired Questions, Actions, and Leaps

✷ Do you have any decisions you're wrestling with right now? Stop and practice the Wise Mind Discernment Process. Remember to Use Your Head to get clear on what the real decision is, Listen to Your Heart to determine what you feel is the right decision, and Trust Your Gut to determine if the decision resonates with you. As you know, you experience the benefits of a process you've read about only after you try it yourself. Try out the Wise Mind Discernment Process a few times to fully experience it and lock it in your memory.

✷ If you haven't already, write down your list of playful distractions that you can use when you need a break. And, remember, those play breaks are allowing valuable work to be done in your nonconscious mind. Studies show that we typically start to lose attention after only ten minutes of interest in a presentation and that attention is critical for learning. So, pay attention (ha ha!) to *your* attention and give yourself a stretch break when your mind starts to wander.

✷ I referred to tarot cards and Angeles Arriens' *The Tarot Handbook* in Chapter Eight. Are you open to 'working' with tarot cards or any of the hundreds of other spiritual, motivational, inspirational, or divination tool card decks? If you are, I highly recommend playing with a few of them to help you tap into your own intuition. Before reading what the author of the card deck has written about the meaning of the card, check in with

your intuition first. Then look at the written explanation.
Do any of the words jump out at you? Why do you think
you were drawn to this card?

Chapter Nine Make the Most of Your Aha! Moments

More than fifteen years ago, Bart was back in school—graduate school—trying to figure out what his next career should be. Upon graduating from the University of Texas with a degree in Communications, Bart had happily started his career in advertising. Like many people, Bart soon realized that his first career wasn't a good fit. So, here he was back on campus, this time exploring the world of physical therapy.

One day, by chance (or was it?), Bart noticed a blind man walking with a guide dog. He'd obviously seen guide dogs in action before, but for some reason, this scene caught his attention. Bart watched as the guide dog carefully led the man down the street, and then did what it was trained to do—it stopped, thereby stopping the man, so he wouldn't fall down the stairs. That's it. But to Bart, it was a 'campus epiphany,' as he calls that experience.

When Bart shared his story with me, he couldn't remember exactly what had made the experience an epiphany, but he described the moment after witnessing the guide dog work as a time when everything slowed way down. All of the pieces of his life seemed to come together to bring a *knowing* of such clarity that he walked away from his plans to pursue a graduate degree in physical therapy.

What makes his experience more amazing is that Bart didn't know specific details about appropriate next steps after the epiphany. He just *knew* that he was meant to work with dogs. Bart's epiphany or aha! moment was so powerful that he *told* his fiancée (now his wife) that he was walking away from all of his education and old plans. No discussion. No hesitation. Bart's new plan was to take a minimum-wage job to work in a kennel until he figured out how he was going to create a sustainable career working with dogs! (How many fiancées or spouses do you know who would still be around six months or more after hearing that kind of 'plan'?)

While Bart can't remember the details of his aha! moment or epiphany from over fifteen years ago, he can remember how compelling it was. It's my belief that the energy from gaining insight or knowledge from all four of his ways of knowing was so strong that he couldn't help but be inspired and changed after the experience.

The great news is that Dog Boy's Dog Ranch is the end result of Bart's willingness to follow his gut until the dream or vision became clear. He and his wife own fifteen acres just outside of Austin and count over seven thousand dogs as their clients. In addition, Bart is a highly sought-after trainer and consultant on "all things dog-related."

Bart gained—in an aha! moment—the wisdom he needed to guide him in the direction he was clearly meant to go. Bart gained a "perspective on life" and felt a "sense of balance and understanding of how the various parts" fit together without having any of the details. Again, the wisdom wasn't a detailed, step-by-step plan, with the end result clearly shown. The wisdom Bart received was the knowing that he loved dogs, even admired them for the work they do, and that he was meant to work with them in some way, shape, or form.

Until One Is Committed

The guidance Bart received was all he needed to confidently make a personal *commitment* to take a giant *leap* in a new direction. He began to move forward with one *inspired* action step at a time. Without consciously realizing it, Bart tapped into cosmic or universal consciousness to guide him. The key for Bart was his ability to stay committed to his dream and not look back, worrying whether or not he'd made the right decision. It's those times of indecision or going back and forth, figuratively wringing our hands that can undo even the best ideas.

When we waver, we shut off access to all of the intelligence around us and listen only to the thoughts in our head and replay past experiences. Again, everything is energy, even your new venture. Focus on keeping your energy moving forward, not zig-zagging back and forth, so that you never really go anywhere.

How can the rest of us find the courage (and ultimate success) that Bart exhibited when he walked away from what he knew, despite the fears and disbelief of his fiancée and others? I believe it's simply a matter of staying open to aha! moments, immediately making a commitment to ourselves to move forward when the aha! or epiphany comes, and replaying the experience in our minds, so we can draw on the power of our aha! when we're challenged by those we love and respect.

The gift of aha! moments is that they're so compelling and filled with such clarity that we're immediately inspired to move in the direction that the wisdom gained in the aha! experience suggests. However, what happens for many of us is that we don't 'lock in' that wisdom, so we can eventually be talked out of what we thought we knew to be true. Family, friends, mounds of data, expert advice—all of this can derail even the most powerful aha! moment if we don't reinforce the experience and expose any interfering beliefs.

Until one is committed, there is hesitancy, the chance to draw back... always ineffectiveness.

W. H. Murray

I have a famous quote from the late explorer W. H. Murray, which I had framed and look at frequently. In it, Murray talks about the power of commitment and the shift in energy that occurs once we've made a firm commitment to a new venture or direction in life. He witnessed this mysterious power at work in his own life. Murray states, "A whole stream of events issues from the decision, raising in one's favor all manner of unforeseen incidents and meetings and material assistance which no one would have dreamt would come his way."[48] Every time I start to lose track of my vision, I re-read that quote and check to see where I've not been committed. When I fix the indecision or lack of commitment, the synchronicities that remind me I'm on the right track return and spur me forward.

It is only when we get stuck in our head going round and round about what others will say, what all of the options are, and what could go wrong that we lose our way. W.H. Murray isn't the only person who confirms the power we all have access to. Patanjali, the author of *Yoga Sutras*, who likely lived a few centuries before Christ, said that when you're truly inspired (perhaps by a strong aha! experience), "Dormant forces, faculties and talents become alive, and you discover yourself to be a greater person by far than you ever dreamed yourself to be."

Be Open to New Possibilities

While Bart's aha! or epiphany was not 'planned,' he'd obviously been seeking a new direction, a new passion or calling, and was **open to new possibilities**. Are you? After all, what do you need aha! moments for if you've no desire to take your life or career to a new level or in a different direction? It's only when we're ready to move away from what we know that the new—the aha!—can come in.

Remember, in Chapter Five, Joe Dispenza emphasized that our bodies are designed to prefer homeostasis and will bring up memories to help generate the thoughts to generate the emotional (chemical) cocktail to keep us feeling the way we've been feeling. In addition, neuroscience shows that the amygdalae (one amygdala is located in the mid or limbic area of each hemisphere of the brain) are a critical part of generating the fear that keeps us safe or in the status quo.

When the amygdalae are damaged, research shows that people experience complete fearlessness, which can ultimately be very dangerous. In daily life, however, most of us need to consciously calm down or work through our fear (at least enough to move forward).

Here Comes Your Inner Critic

No matter how inspiring your aha! experience might be, there will be a part of you that will do everything it can to keep you where you are. Yes, the dreaded inner critic shows up. And, it's very, very smart. When you're off in the wilderness exploring a new, undiscovered jungle, the power of this intelligent part of you is a good thing. When you're simply trying to find your ideal career or mate, it's not so good.

Thankfully, now that we have a better understanding of the biology behind the strength of the inner critic, it's easier to direct it rather than let it direct you. Imagine your inner critic (working with your body's chemical cocktail needs and the amygdalae in your brain) bringing up memories, bringing in friends, family, and co-workers, and making you aware of research—all designed to dissuade you from your goal. The key is to not take this personally. This inner voice isn't the real you. The more you're able to step back and recognize that it's simply doing its job, the less control your inner critic will have over your thoughts and actions.

So, borrowing from that trite phrase "if you can't beat them, join them," one of the best ways to outsmart your amygdalae and your body's chemical cocktail is to embrace how you're wired. We've all heard about how lobsters, crabs, and frogs won't jump out of the pot if you start with cold water and slowly—very slowly—turn up the heat. Use that same method of slow yet steady progress to keep your body and mind from overreacting to a new direction you want to move in.

Bart didn't take his epiphany of working with dogs and immediately pull all of his money out the bank, drop everything, and create his own dog kennel. He stayed focused on his vision, and took calculated risks. Yes, it was a big step to work for minimum wage at a kennel, but it wasn't nearly the risk that leaping into creating his own kennel would have been at the time.

There will be times when you'll feel that you can take a big leap toward fulfilling the vision of your aha! moment. If you've checked in with all of your ways of knowing and it feels right to you, then fully commit yourself and go for it. However, there will also be many times when your confidence will waver. Check in. If a step you've set yourself up to take feels uncomfortable, break it into smaller steps and look at what underlying beliefs (which your inner critic will use) are coming up to keep you at status quo.

The more I understand the power of the body and mind to wreak havoc on the best-laid plans if they're too far out of our comfort zone, the more inclined I am to ignore the traditional advice to "feel the fear and do it anyway," or "just do it." A more fitting slogan for the way we're designed might be the statement: "Feel the fear, change your thoughts (and therefore emotions), then confidently move forward one step at a time." I know. It doesn't have the same ring to it as those other statements, and might be a bit long, but for me, that's what works. Go with what works for you.

Ready.

Fire.

Aim.

T. Harv Eker

Take *Inspired* Action

You may have heard that *inspired* means 'in spirit,' but do you apply that understanding to the actions you take on a daily basis? Are you *only* taking inspired action? It's been noted many times that the Western world prides itself on being action-oriented versus the more reflective and receptive Eastern world. As we better understand the power of energy fields and the collective unconscious, it's easier to understand how growing up in one culture or another would influence your predisposition toward action. For most of us in the West, our optimal performance in life will occur when we reduce our focus on action and balance it with time for quiet and reflection.

Please don't misunderstand me. I love action and am more inclined to follow the Nike exhortation 'just do it' than is prudent. And in times of indecision, I believe my mother's advice of "just make a move, even if it's wrong" is brilliant. In fact, T. Harv Eker of Peak Potentials and author of *Secrets of the Millionaire Mind* first made me aware of this slogan: Ready. Fire. Aim.[49] We can spend too much time 'aiming' and getting it right and miss our chance at the target all together.

When I talk about waiting to take action until you feel inspired, I'm referring to allowing for time to tap into your unlimited spiritual or creative energy, your intelligence, and the energy and intelligence of the universe. It doesn't matter whether 'universe' means God to you or the energy zipping around in all of that not-so-empty space we exist in. Taking a moment to check in with your Energetic System of Knowing enables you to determine the ideal time to begin a project, make a call, or set a deadline.

Even if you think it's a bunch of hooey that we can tap into a universal intelligence, consider tapping into your own thoughts, emotions, and beliefs about the action. Yes, there are times when we've got a tight deadline or an emergency, so we must dive in and make something happen. But much of the time, we can *choose* when and how we take action. Taking time to create the ideal action scenario for you enables you to leverage all of the resources at your disposal, including the unseen, but no less real, intelligence around you.

Just a moment spent checking in to determine how and when you feel great about taking a step can pay huge dividends.

....

Inspired Questions, Actions, and Leaps

❉ Where in your work or your life have you failed to make a commitment to something you were inspired about? Is there any vision or dream that you need to re-commit yourself to?

❉ What actions tell you that you're truly committed to something? Are you consistently taking those action steps when it comes to your top goals or dreams?

❉ Make a commitment to check in regularly with yourself to 'scan' your mindset and your recent actions. If a reminder of your commitment is needed, do what you need to do to consciously re-commit.

❉ Remember you don't have to make your dream a reality all on your own. W. H. Murray states that "A whole stream of events issues from the decision, raising in one's favor all manner of unforeseen incidents and meetings and material assistance which no one would have dreamt would come his way."[50]

    ✳ Are you trying to do everything yourself? Can you press the pause button on your work or your life for a moment and be a witness to all of the help that's coming your way? I've found that the more I express gratitude for the help I'm receiving, the more help seems to show up.

* When we're constantly in action mode, we don't allow the flow to occur. It doesn't always take much time, but it does take a bit of time for things to line up for you once you've made the commitment. If you jump into a flurry of motion, you may miss some important signs along the way—signs that might easily guide you to what you want.

* Remember Bart's story? He didn't know the whole plan or what the end result would be. He just kept moving forward, slowly but surely. The ideas and next steps revealed themselves to him in perfect timing. This same process of having your dream slowly unfold can happen for you.

....

Need an Aha! Moment? Try This!

Wear a Different Hat. Similar to the suggestion to imagine what a valued mentor or spiritual leader might do in your situation (Chapter Seven's "Try This" activity), but even more of a stretch is to look at your question or challenge from the point of view of cartoon or movie characters like Batman, Harry Potter, Wonder Woman, or even Mickey Mouse or Daffy Duck. The more exaggerated the personality of the character, the better. The idea is to shake things up and get out of your comfort zone and normal ways of thinking. I believe it was Albert Einstein who noted that the same mind that created the problem can't solve it. So, you need an expanded mind to experience the aha! or solution.

Clients have felt silly, had fun, and experienced profound insights while playing a game of moving from one costume prop or picture of a character or job role (policeman, cowboy, CEO, nurse, queen, marketing manager, king, or pirate, for example). Each time they stop at a 'station,' they put on a different 'hat' and look at their question from that character's perspective. What character is completely opposite you in personality type? That's likely the first 'hat' you should put on.

Aha!

Chapter Ten **Claim Your Brilliance**

Greg (his real name) flipped through his weekly calendar, looking at, but not really seeing, his sales appointments for the week. He felt uncomfortable, irritable, and edgy, but that was nothing new. For the last four years, after a debilitating 2000 that included finding out that his cousin had brain cancer, watching his life savings disappear in a stock market fiasco, and losing his last grandparent to old age, his dad to a stroke, and another cousin to a horrible accident, Greg had been on a steep downhill slide. Drinking through the nights and using his natural charm to plow through most of the days, Greg's life had been a wild emotional roller coaster ride that took its toll on his career and love life.

Even when Greg tried to start fresh in a new city and a new job in 2003, trouble seemed to follow him. The drinking continued and one night led him to be in the wrong place at the wrong time. He was lucky to still be alive after a vicious gang attack. Thankfully, his survival from the attack and a wonderful new relationship got him to realize his drinking was a problem.

"Geez, what a mess my life still is," thought Greg, during a free moment at work during the spring of 2004. He shook himself out of his depression and concentrated on finishing his job. When he got home that night, Greg decided that enough was enough. It was time to make a change.

Perhaps the idea began to blossom in Greg after the profound experience of Reiki his ex-girlfriend had given him. Greg could still remember the warm healing energy and the sense that someone was "knocking on his heart." Or, maybe it was all of his prayers asking "please show me my path." Whatever it was, the nagging irritation, the inner voice telling him that something wasn't right, wouldn't let him go. That spring night, Greg had an aha! realization. It wasn't a 'hit-you-over-the-head' experience. It was a slow build-up of experiences that opened Greg up to the realization that he wasn't meant to spend another moment sitting behind a desk or drowning his sorrows in booze.

He quit his job, sold most of his belongings, and stored the rest in his aunt's garage. In the summer of 2004, Greg set out on a trip along with two friends, a couple who planned to travel the first few months of the trip with him. Greg decided to bring a $400 Olympus camera to commemorate the journey and maybe make a little extra cash selling his photos over the Internet. He'd had a love for photography in high school, but had let it go to focus on his business studies at Baylor University. With a little bit of money, the camera, and a few clothes, Greg and his friends started their adventure by going east, to Turkey.

Once he got on the road, Greg felt better, more at peace and confident than he had in years. This was the right next stage of his life at the right time. After four months of traveling together, the friends parted ways with Greg, as planned, with each choosing to explore a different part of the world. Greg continued on into Thailand (he was there during the tsunami, but thankfully away from the coast) and Vietnam, taking photos of whatever captured his heart. In fact, the phrase

"Something always captures me first…" became his motto to describe why he chose to photograph something or someone.

Deep in the northern highlands of Vietnam, he was 'captured' by a Hmong blanket weaver. Her hands were two different colors. One was dyed green and the other blue. Greg felt compelled to take a photograph of her amazing hands.

There are people who make a living reading the shape, lines, and swirls of hands to reveal life patterns, life history, and provide a glimpse of your life's path or passion. But this time, those beautiful hands of a hard-working woman ultimately revealed Greg's life path. For that one image—the Blanket Weaver, among others—so captivated friends and family, and later strangers, that he realized his gift, his passion, was photography. Greg now travels the country sharing his photography and story and will continue to travel for inspiration. (www.gregdavis-photography.com)

Greg's journey wasn't easy, and it didn't hit him over the head, but some unseen force kept pointing him on the way. He slowly but surely started paying attention to the synchronicities or meaningful coincidences.

While the trip was a profound experience, Greg needed to get back to reality and make some money to pay his bills. When he arrived in Austin after his adventure, Greg found that he'd only sold about $500 worth of images he'd posted on his website during the year he was gone—hardly enough to live on. So, Greg initially ignored his gift, not seeing it for what it was, and got a job. It took a Canadian friend he'd met while traveling in Australia, who came to visit and see the rest of his photographs, to tell him how talented he was. He still didn't believe it. After all, she was his friend. So, guess what? 'Fate' interfered again.

Walking down 6th street in Austin, Greg was showing his friend the city. They walked by an art fair. His friend grabbed Greg and said "Let's check it out. Maybe you can sell your photography here." Reluctantly Greg followed her in. They met the organizer, who invited Greg to participate at the next art fair. So Greg spent a few hundred dollars framing his pictures, and getting set up to sell them. He made over $250 on the first day he exhibited his work and slowly built up his business in his spare time. In fact, after that initial taste of success, Greg set a goal of paying for his world travels within one year. The week before the year was up, he paid off his trip! That gave him the courage to quit his day job (again) and pursue his photography business.

No more desks. No more offices. No more paper-pushing. There's nothing wrong with any of it. That world challenged, educated, fed, and clothed Greg for ten years and for the first year he got back. It ultimately gave Greg the savings to start his life-changing trip and career and the knowledge to manage his own business and sell his photography. His corporate jobs just weren't what he was meant to do for the rest of his life. Greg now lives by an anonymous quote he found that says exactly what he learned: "There's no reason to look back. You're not headed that way." Someone, some innate intelligence, or some cosmic conscious-ness knew that and guided Greg. Even when he was lost and at his most depressed, he was still shown the signs. When you feel lost or stuck, remember guidance or next steps are still coming your way. All you have to do is pay close attention.

Like Greg, you have access to unseen, but no less powerful, wisdom to guide (or nag) you on your path. It's rarely possible for us to imagine the twists and turns our lives will take and why we're compelled to do something. Yet when we honor our aha! moments and the intelligence that flows through us, we claim our brilliance. Otherwise, we're merely shells of who we could be, limping along, trying our best, working so hard, but still barely tapping into our potential.

It takes courage to acknowledge your brilliance and follow it regardless of what those around you say. The good news is that you have all of the courage you need. It's simply a choice you make: to trust yourself or not.

Follow Your Lightning Bolt

There are thousands of thoughts, hundreds of tasks, and many people that will try to claim your attention and your energy, but when the lightning bolt of an aha! comes, it's time to tune them all out and follow your aha! Remember that you are uniquely gifted because all of your experiences have created a unique brain and a unique way of interpreting information. No one else will follow through on your insight or inspiration like you will. Trust that if the lightning bolt strikes, it strikes for a reason.

Because you are an energetic being, your energy is blocked or diminished when you try to shut down or ignore the inspiration you receive. Many of us ignore our aha! experiences or unconsciously avoid them because we're afraid of the possible changes in our lives and the lives of those we love if we honor the inspiration. Yet when you honor the aha's that come along, they guide you to the right next step at the right time.

There are thousands of thoughts, hundreds of tasks, and many people that will try to claim your attention and your energy, but when the lightning bolt of an aha! comes, it's time to tune them all out and follow your aha!

Dianna Amorde

The Journey

Of course, the first step on the journey toward your dream or goal can be the most difficult, especially when it's inspired by an aha! moment. Like intuition, you don't know how or why you *know* that you're supposed to start on this new adventure, you just know. Unfortunately, family, friends, and co-workers can't experience the sudden knowing that you do, so they may do all that they can to hold you back. Sometimes it's in concern for you and sometimes it's in fear for how they'll fit in with the new you.

Poet Mary Oliver addresses the challenge of striking out in a new direction you feel called to go, even when family, friends, and the advice of experts tell you not to do it.

The Journey[51]

One day you finally knew
what you had to do, and began,
though the voices around you
kept shouting
their bad advice—
though the whole house
began to tremble
and you felt the old tug
at your ankles.
'Mend my life!'
each voice cried.
But you didn't stop.
You knew what you had to do,
though the wind pried
with its stiff fingers
at the very foundations—
though their melancholy
was terrible.

It was already late
enough, and a wild night,
and the road full of fallen
branches and stones.
But little by little,
as you left their voices behind,
the stars began to burn
through the sheets of clouds,
and there was a new voice,
which you slowly
recognized as your own,
that kept you company
as you strode deeper and deeper
into the world,
determined to do
the only thing you could do—
determined to save
the only life that you could save.

—*Mary Oliver*

This poem moves me. It speaks to that powerful knowing that comes over you when you've found the answer you seek and you feel compelled to move forward despite all of the obstacles thrown in your way. Yet most of us have those dark moments when we doubt our vision or the aha! experience we've had, especially when loved ones don't understand and are frightened by the changes in us. They ask, "Where is the person I used to know?"

In those dark moments, *The Journey* comforts me, reminding me that I'm not selfish or crazy and not alone. However, because I haven't had much experience reading and discussing poetry, my deepest appreciation for *The Journey* came after reading Roger Housden's interpretation of it in his inspiring book, *Ten Poems to Change Your Life*.

(If you aren't comfortable with poetry, I highly recommend his work. Housden will give you a new appreciation for the remarkable talent of poets like Mary Oliver). Housden shared how Oliver's poem spoke to changes he'd just made in his life:

> When I first read this poem I had just landed in San Francisco from London. That one reading made my hair stand on end. It confirmed the rightness of all that had just happened in my life. A few months earlier, I had woken up one morning and knew I should leave my native country of England and go and live in America. Just like that. ***Rather than a decision, it was like recognizing something whose time had come.*** Everything needed to change, and the time was now.[52]

Housden goes on to say that like his move to America, these 'just like that' changes are really gestating within us for months or even years. But when we're ready, they hit us. "One day, this kind of knowing just happens. It happens outside of ordinary time. It swoops in sideways, at an odd angle, and like the swallow, it is the harbinger of new things, a new caste of mind."[53]

When this aha! experience happens, we immediately have a choice to follow our inspirations or not. However, it's not really a choice. Our lives will never be as happy, healthy, rewarding, or successful if we ignore the call. "It was already late enough," Mary Oliver says. To ignore it or to wait is to further delay your vision, your happiness. But the challenges are many. Loved ones, co-workers, bosses, community leaders will all try to 'tug at your ankle' to keep you from changing. Not because they don't want you to be happy, but because they're human and looking out for themselves. Just as our bodies resist change, so do theirs. And they don't have the benefit of the jolt of energy and vision you have to guide you past the fears and status quo.

This is your life. You're the only one who has the unique combination of an evolved brain that brings in all of your past experiences, a body that reflects what's true for you today, emotions that tell you when the direction you're heading is right for you at this time, and the spirit to shout 'Yes!' when you're following the path that is meant for you.

> You are far more brilliant than you think you are, so trust yourself and take an inspired leap toward your dreams.

Your Energetic System of Knowing will reveal to you all of the answers you need when you need them. All you need to do is keep the channels open and flowing.

* **Mental** – Your intellectual abilities are great and can't help but bring all of your experiences and knowledge from birth, along with the beliefs that arose from those experiences, to every decision you make.

* **Emotional** – Your emotions are neither good nor bad. They are signals telling you that you're honoring who you are and moving forward on your life path or thinking, speaking, or doing something that doesn't honor who you are.

* **Physical** – Your body can appear to be working against you when you're making a shift in consciousness and in your life, but listen to its wisdom. It can reveal what's in your nonconscious mind or in the energy around you, but not yet in your conscious awareness.

* **Spiritual** – You have access to all of the intelligence that came before you, is here now, and will be here in the future. Your soul accesses this wisdom and knows who

you truly are. It will always guide you in the direction that supports you.

Remember, It's All Energy

When you remember that all of you and all of this world is flowing energy, then you can handle the challenges that come your way and heed the call of your aha! moments. Ask yourself on a daily basis, am I in the flow? Am I going with *my* flow? Just like you don't want a drain to back up, you don't want to block the flow of intelligence to you and stifle your energy.

1. Energy is meant to flow. A build-up of stagnant or blocked energy may stay blocked for years, or may lead to an eruption, which allows the energy to flow again. In either case, you're not operating optimally.

   * Your Energetic Guidance System can't work effectively if one or more of the channels is blocked, leading to 'flooding' your system with backed-up energy.

   * Emotional outbursts come from energy that hasn't been dealt with.

   * If energy wants to move and it's not safe or compassionate (or legal) to express your emotions, then physically exercise them out of your system.

2. Energy can be transferred from you to someone or something else and vice versa.

   * Protect your energy. Be careful what you allow in and what you send out. Don't be an energy vampire, draining the energy out of people, and be careful to avoid people who drain you.

3. Energy comes in a wide variety of forms, including yours.

* You are a beautiful, unique human being and spirit AND you're an energy field. Try to see your experiences as a reflection of the energy your 'field' is sending out into the world. This makes it easier to detach from mistakes and challenges and look at the messages you've been consciously and nonconsciously sending. Have you been clear about what you want? Could your mistake or challenge have come from a mixed message?

* Have compassion for yourself. Perhaps an error you made came from an attack of your pain-body or a spike in your chemical cocktail. Perhaps you were in your head and had forgotten to check in with your heart. Whatever the error, take the learning, adjust your energy accordingly, and move on. Keep the energy moving.

4. Energy can never be created or destroyed. It just is. (This is the First Law of Thermodynamics).

* You have access to all of the information (energy) that has come before you and has been thought to date. You may even have access to information about the future. (I think so).

Something Wonderful Is About to Happen

I have a bumper sticker with "Something Wonderful is About to Happen" on it.[54] Live your life as if something wonderful—an aha! moment—is about to happen. Act as if. Can you imagine starting each day with the knowing that something wonderful is about to happen? That the answers you need are coming today, this very minute.

You create the 'something wonderful.' You do it each time you claim your brilliance and honor your unique wisdom and the way you filter or process universal intelligence. No one can see the world you see. No one. So, no one else knows what is best for you in any given moment. No parent. No boss. No spouse. No child. No physician. No politician. No one else can tell you what is best for you.

That doesn't mean throwing responsibility, caring, and compassion out the window or breaking the law. It means taking responsibility for all that you create and all that you decide. Your wisest decisions will be made when you activate your wise mind and check in with your Energetic System of Knowing. Your worst decisions will be made when you 'shoot from the hip,' exploding in anger or rage because you've been oblivious to all of your inner guidance, or you listen to everyone else's voice except your own. It's your choice.

Because we're each unique and connected at the same time, each time you honor who you are and act from your highest good, you raise your consciousness … and you raise mine. And hers. And his. And theirs.

It's not always easy, though, to honor the jolt of energy of an aha! moment or the inner voice that softly, but persistently, nudges you with hunches, dreams, and synchronicities. So when you are trapped in your head and feel lost or afraid to move forward, ask for a helping hand to reach down and pull you up. Maybe it will be the blanket weaver's hand. Maybe it will be mine. Maybe it will be an angel's. Hold your hand up. Ask for a lift and *feel* the energy of someone pulling you up. That, my friend, is the power of working from your wise mind, living from one aha! moment to the next, and opening to and accepting your energetic connection to the world.

So what wise decisions will you make today?

....

Inspired Questions, Actions, and Leaps

✳ Is there a dream or aha! insight you have that you haven't acted on? Why not? What would happen if you resurrected it and began to take a step toward it (just a small step)?

✳ "Something Wonderful is About to Happen." What? Where in your life are you ready for something wonderful to happen? What steps could you take to help the universe create that 'something wonderful' experience?

✳ Remember the 'until one is committed' truth that W.H. Murray offered. Are you truly committed to welcoming an aha! moment or something wonderful?

✳ What journey have you been afraid to begin? Perhaps you think you're simply being prudent because the timing isn't right for your family, for the economy, or for your company. Perhaps you believe you need a bit more money in the savings account or another year of study. If you've had the aha! experience, if you remember your lightning bolt of knowing, then you've received the signal that you have all you need at this moment to get started. Could fear of change be getting in the way? If so, what's one teeny-tiny step you can take to begin your journey? Remember, you're in charge, so you can take as long as you'd like to make the journey to your dream. So, why not get started right now?

✳ Do you have a muse? Do you have someone who inspires you and believes in you? Greg had his friend from Canada who gave him the big push to do something with his photography. I bet you have someone around you who can do that for you. If not, send me an email. I'll be happy to get you started. I took an inspired leap and created a new career and happier life. Now it's time for you to. And if you've already done it, please share your story with me and your friends, so others will be inspired too.

Appendix A Bibliography and
Recommended Reading

Arntz, William, Betsy Chasse, and Mark Vicente. *What the Bleep Do We Know!?* Deerfield Beach, FL: Health Communications, Inc., 2005.

Arrien, Angeles. *The Tarot Handbook: Practical Applications of Ancient Visual Symbols.* New York: Jeremy P. Tarcher/Putnam, 1987.

Bench, Douglas. *Mind Your Brain!* (Audio CD ROM program). McIntosh, FL: Science for Success Academy, 2005.

Biello, David. "Searching for God in the Brain," *Scientific American Mind*, October/November 2007.

Bradley, Raymond Trevor. *The Psychophysiology of Entrepreneurial Intuition: A Quantum-Holographic Theory.* Institute for Whole Social Science; Institute of HeartMath, CA, USA, and e-Motion Institute, Auckland, New Zealand, reported in: Proceedings of the Third AGSE International Entrepreneurship Research Exchange, February 8-10, 2006.

Branan, Nicole. "Unconscious Decisions," *Scientific American Mind*, August/September 2008.

Brown, Harriet. "The Other Brain Also Deals With Many Woes." *The New York Times*, August 23, 2005. Retrieved September 4, 2008 from http://www.nytimes.com/2005/08/23/health/23gut.html

Burton, Robert. *On Being Certain.* New York: St. Martin's Press, 2008.

Claxton, Guy. *Hare Brain, Tortoise Mind.* New York: HarperCollins, 1997.

Cooper, Robert. *The Other 90%.* New York: Three Rivers Press, 2001.

Dietz, Lisa. *Wise Mind* (http://www.dbtselfhelp.com). Lisa Dietz, 2003.

Dispenza, Joe. *Evolve Your Brain.* Deerfield Beach, FL: Health Communications, Inc., 2007.

Dobbs, David. "Eric Kandel: From Mind to Brain and Back Again," *Scientific American Mind*, October/November 2007.

Dyer, Wayne. *The Power of Intention.* Carlsbad, CA: Hay House, Inc., 2004.

Edwards, Betty. *The New Drawing on the Right Side of the Brain.* New York: Jeremy P. Tarcher/Putnam, 1999.

Eiffert, Stephen. *Cross-Train Your Brain.* New York: AMACOM, 1999.

Eker, T. Harv. *Secrets of the Millionaire Mind.* New York: HarperBusiness, 2005.

Emery, Marcia. *Intuition Workbook.* Englewood Cliffs, NJ: Prentice Hall, 1994.

Gawain, Shakti. *Creative Visualization.* New York: Bantam Books, a division of Random House Inc., 1978.

Gladwell, Malcolm. *Blink.* New York: Little Brown and Company, 2005.

Goleman, Daniel. *Emotional Intelligence.* New York: Bantam Books, 1995.

Goleman, Daniel. *Social Intelligence.* New York: Bantam Dell, 2006.

Goleman, Daniel, Richard Boyatzis, and Annie McKee. *Primal Leadership.* Boston: Harvard Business School Publishing, 2002.

Hawkins, David. *Power Versus Force: The Hidden Determinants of Human Behavior.* Sedona, AZ: Veritas Publishing, 1995, 1998.

Hay, Louise L. *Heal Your Body.* Carlsbad, CA: Hay House, Inc., 1988.

Hendricks, Gay, and Kate Ludeman. *The Corporate Mystic.* New York: Bantam Books, 1996.

Housden, Roger. *Ten Poems to Change Your Life.* New York: Harmony Books, 2001.

Hunt, Valerie. *Infinite Mind: The Science of Human Vibrations of Consciousness.* Malibu, CA: Malibu Publishing Company, 1996.

Jaworski, Joseph. *Synchronicity: The Inner Path to Leadership.* San Francisco: Berrett-Koehler Publishers, 1998.

Katie, Byron. *Loving What Is.* New York: Harmony Books, 2002.

Klein, Gary. *The Power of Intuition* (formerly titled *Intuition at Work*). New York: Random House, 2003.

Lilienfeld, Scott O. and Hal Arkowitz. "Uncovering Brainscams," *Scientific American Mind*, February/March 2008.

Lipton, Bruce. *The Biology of Belief.* Santa Rosa, CA: Mountain of Love/ Elite Books, 2005.

Loehr, Jim, and Tony Schwartz. *The Power of Full Engagement.* New York: Free Press, 2003.

McCraty, Rollin, Mike Atkinson, and Raymond Trevor Bradley. "Electrophysiological Evidence of Intuition: Part 1. The Surprising Role of the Heart." *The Journal of Alternative and Complementary Medicine*, Volume 10, Number 1, 2004.

McCraty, Rollin, Mike Atkinson, and Raymond Trevor Bradley. "Electrophysiological Evidence of Intuition: Part 2. A System-Wide Process?" *The Journal of Alternative and Complementary Medicine*, Volume 10, Number 2, 2004.

McCraty, Rollin, Raymond Trevor Bradley, and Dana Tomasino. "The Resonant Heart." *Shift: At the Frontiers of Consciousness*, Institute of Noetic Sciences, December 2004 – February 2005.

McTaggart, Lynne. *The Field*. New York: HarperCollins Publishers, 2002.

McTaggart, Lynne. *The Intention Experiment: Using Your Thoughts to Change Your Life and the World*. New York: Free Press, a division of Simon & Schuster, 2007.

Medina, John. *Brain Rules*. Seattle: Pear Press, 2008.

Mitchell, Edgar. *Edgar Mitchell's Epiphany* (http://www.noetic.org). Institute of Noetic Sciences, 2009.

Murray, William H. *The Scottish Himalayan Expedition*. London: J.M. Dent & Sons, 1951.

Myss, Caroline. *Anatomy of the Spirit: The Seven Stages of Power and Healing*. New York: Harmony Books, 1996.

Myss, Caroline. *Sacred Contracts: Awakening Your Divine Potential*, New York: Harmony Books, 2001.

Myss, Caroline, and Norm Shealy. *The Science of Medical Intuition*. Boulder: Sounds True, Inc., 2002.

National Science Foundation (2008, June 6). "Plastic Brain Outsmarts Experts: Training Can Increase Fluid Intelligence, Once Thought To Be Fixed At Birth." *ScienceDaily*. Retrieved August 5, 2008 from http://www.sciencedaily.com/releases/2008/06/080605163804.htm.

Nelson, Roger. *Global Consciousness Project Web Site* (http://noosphere. princeton.edu/). 2008

Oliver, Mary. *Dream Work.* New York: Grove/Atlantic, 1986.

Orloff, Judith. *Positive Energy: 10 Extraordinary Prescriptions for Transforming Fatigue, Stress, and Fear into Vibrance, Strength, & Love.* New York: Harmony Books, 2004.

Parikh, Jagdish, Fred Neubauer, and Alden Lank. *Intuition: The New Frontier of Management.* Cambridge: Blackwell Publishers Inc, 1996.

Pease, Allan, and Barbara Pease. *The Definitive Book of Body Language.* New York: Bantam Dell, a division of Random House, 2004.

Pert, Candace. *Everything You Need to Know to Feel Go(o)d.* Carlsbad, CA: Hay House, Inc., 2006.

Pink, Daniel. *A Whole New Mind.* New York: Riverhead Books, 2005.

Restak, Richard. *The Naked Brain.* New York: Harmony Books, 2006.

Restak, Richard. *The New Brain.* New York: Rodale Press, 2003.

Restak, Richard. *Mozart's Brain and the Fighter Pilot: Unleashing Your Brain's Potential.* New York: Harmony Books, 2001.

Robinson, Lynn. *Trust Your Gut: How the Power of Intuition Can Grow Your Business.* Chicago: Kaplan Publishing, 2006.

Schulz, Mona Lisa. *Awakening Intuition.* New York: Harmony Books, 1998.

Senge, Peter. *The Fifth Discipline: The Art and Practice of The Learning Organization.* New York: Doubleday, a division of Random House, 1990.

Stickgold, Robert and Jeffrey M. Ellenbogen. "Quiet! Sleeping Brain at Work," *Scientific American Mind*, August/September 2008.

Taylor, Jill Bolte. *My Stroke of Insight.* New York: Viking Penguin, a division of Penguin Group, 2006.

Tolle, Eckhart. *The Power of Now: A Guide to Spiritual Enlightenment.* Novato, CA and Vancouver, BC: New World Library and Namaste Publishing, 1999.

Tolle, Eckhart. *A New Earth: Awakening Your Life's Purpose.* New York: Plume, a member of Penguin Group, 2005.

University of Michigan (2008, May 6). "Brain-training To Improve Memory Boots Fluid Intelligence." *ScienceDaily.* Retrieved August 5, 2008 from http://www.sciencedaily.com/releases/2008/05/08050575642.htm.

Wheatley, Margaret. *Leadership and the New Science.* San Francisco: Berrett-Koehler Publishers, Inc., 1994.

Williams, Roy. *Free the Beagle: A Journey to Destinae.* Atlanta: Bard Press, 2002.

Zohar, Danah. *Rewiring the Corporate Brain.* San Francisco: Berrett-Koehler Publishers, 1997.

Zukav, Gary. *The Dancing Wu Li Master: An Overview of the New Physics.* New York: William Morrow and Company, 1979.

Zukav, Gary. *The Seat of the Soul.* New York: Fireside, 1989.

Zukav, Gary and Linda Francis. *The Heart of the Soul: Emotional Awareness.* New York: Free Press, a division of Simon & Schuster, 2001.

Appendix B **Additional Resources**

Check Out These Websites to Expand Your Awareness of How We and the World Work

The Global Consciousness Project: http://noosphere.princeton.edu/

* Also called the EGG Project, it is an international collaboration of scientists, engineers, artists, and others.

* Asks the question, "What is the nature of global consciousness?"

The Institute of HeartMath: http://www.heartmath.org/

* Offers a variety of products and techniques for helping you to reduce the effects of stress and bring your heartbeat to its optimal rate.

* Includes a rich source of information about the latest research on the role the heart plays in many aspects of our lives.

The Global Coherence Project: http://www.glcoherence.org/

* Affiliated with The Institute of HeartMath, but with its own rich source of information, including a fascinating report called *The Power of Emotion* (© 2008 HeartMath LLC).

The Institute of Noetic Sciences: http://www.ions.org/

✱ The Institute conducts and sponsors leading-edge research that adheres to the principles of scientific rigor, but may be in areas not focused on by conventional science. The areas researched include the potentials and powers of consciousness, including perceptions, beliefs, attention, intention, and intuition.

The World Wide Tipping Point Project:
http://www.worldwidetippingpoint.com

✱ Started by Todd Goldfarb and based on the belief that the personal energy of commitment of individuals around the world can change the world and move us toward peace.

Create or Color Mandalas For Intuitive Processing, Healing, or Expression

The Mandala Healing Kit: Using Sacred Symbols for Spiritual and Emotional Healing by Judith Cornell, Ph.D., © 2005 Judith Cornell. Published by Sounds True, www.soundstrue.com.

Coloring Mandalas 1: For Insight, Healing, and Self-Expression by Susanne F. Fincher, © 2000 Susanne F. Fincher. Published by Shambhala Publications, Inc., www.shambhala.com or www.creatingmandalas.com.

Develop Your Power to Visualize Success

Download the "Find the Answer You Seek" visualization described in Chapter Eight: http://www.ahamomentsbook.com/visualization.

Envision Your Way to Success audio CD by Dianna Amorde, © 2008 by Dianna Amorde. http://www.inspiredleap.com The CD contains four powerful guided visualizations and over 30 minutes of inspiration, stories, and tips about how to develop your power to visualize.

Creative Visualization, book or audio CD, by Shakti Gawain. © 1992 by Shakti Gawain. Published by New World Library.

Infinite Possibilities: The Art of Living Your Dreams audio CD by Mike Dooley, © TUT ® Enterprises, Inc. Published by TUT ® Enterprises, Inc.

The Joy of Visualization: 75 Creative Ways to Enhance Your Life by Valerie Wells, © 1990 by Valerie Wells. Published by Chronicle Books.

Develop Self-Awareness and Intuition Via Card Decks

The Tarot Handbook: Practical Applications of Ancient Visual Symbols by Angeles Arrien, © 1987, 1997 by Angeles Arrien. Published by Jeremy P. Tarcher/Putnam, a member of Penguin (USA) Inc.

THOTH Tarot Deck, Designed by Aleister Crowley and Painted by Lady Frieda Harris (The tarot deck featured in *The Tarot Handbook: Practical Application of Ancient Visual Symbols*), © 1978 by U.S. Games Systems, Inc. and Samuel Weiser, Inc.

Ask Your Guides Oracle Cards by Sonia Choquette, © 2005 by Sonia Choquette www.soniachoquette.com. Published by Hay House, Inc., www.hayhouse.com.

Healing With The Angels Oracle Cards by Doreen Virtue, Ph.D., © 1999 by Doreen Virtue, www.AngelTherapy.com. Published by Hay House, Inc. www.hayhouse.com.

Also, any other card decks that appeal to you. The idea is to play with the idea that your energy enables you to select the appropriate card or message for you at any given time and to allow yourself to intuit what the meaning of the card is *before* you read the author's interpretation. Think of it as warm-up exercises for your intuitive muscles.

Learn More About Wise Mind (as used in Dialectical Behavior Therapy)

www.dbtselfhelp.com/html/wise_mind.html

Other possible sources that I have not personally reviewed

The Dialectical Behavior Therapy Skills Workbook by Matthew McKay, Jeffery C. Wood, Jeffrey Brantley

Article on DBT and Wise Mind: http://stanford.wellsphere. com/mental-health-article/dialectical-behavior-therapy-dbt-core-mindfulness/527491

Or if you think you may desire professional help in moving into wise mind or in letting go of old beliefs, contact a psychiatrist or psychologist:

American Psychiatric Association, www.psych.org

American Psychological Association, www.apa.org

Shift Your Thinking (Letting Go of Old Beliefs)

Check out The Work® of Byron Katie at www.thework.com or read her powerful book, *Loving What Is*, © 2002 by Byron Kathleen Mitchell. Published by Harmony Books, a division of Random House, Inc.

Shift Your Thinking Via the Power of Poetry

Read any of Roger Housden's poetry anthologies, especially *Ten Poems to Change Your Life*.

Read Bill Moyers' *Fooling With Words: A Celebration of Poets and Their Craft*. Moyers makes poetry accessible to those of us who have bad memories from high school English classes.

Learn More About the Work of Those Who Shared Their Stories

Photographer Mary Ann Halpin (from Chapter Four) inspires women and men to claim their power, acknowledge their inner glow, or let their authentic selves shine through. I've had the privilege of becoming a Fearless Woman. To find out more about what being a Fearless Woman means, check out her photography. www.maryannhalpin.com

Diane Graden (from Chapter Six), Owner of Frames of Reference, an Austin-area mobile framing company that beautifully frames your treasures. She's also using her intuitive heart to bring together local artists and corporations to publicly display the creative talent of Austin. www.framesofreference.biz

Barbara Metzger (from Chapter Seven) still listens to her intuition to prepare a comprehensive picture of potential employees' strengths and challenges for small business owners via a mix of assessments. Check out her business, Maximize, at www.maxproductivity.com.

Sara Blakely (from Chapter Eight), the founder of Spanx, a line of women's hosiery and undergarments, shares her inspiring story and the work of her foundation on the Spanx website. www.spanx.com

Dog Boy, trainer and expert in all things dog related, Bart Emken (from Chapter Nine) taps into his Channels of Knowing to sense what's best for any dog who comes to Dog Boys Dog Ranch. www.dogboys.com.

Photographer Greg Davis (see a picture of the blanket weaver's hands—from Chapter Ten—at Greg's website) travels the country sharing his captivating images and his inspiring story. From Myanmar to Morocco, something captures him, and we get to experience that magic in his photographs. www.gregdavisphotography.com

Endnotes

1. Source: *Webster's New World College Dictionary,* Fourth Edition (Foster City, CA: IDG Books Worldwide, Inc., 2000).

2. I first heard the term 'nonconscious mind' while listening to Doug Bench's *Mind Your Brain!* audio program. (Science for Success Academy, 2005). Most recently, in *On Being Certain: Believing You Are Right Even When You're Not,* by Robert A. Burton, M.D. differentiates between the conscious mind and the unconscious mind, with no mention of the subconscious mind (pp. 128-136).

3. One of my favorite books on the importance of developing the right hemisphere of the brain is Daniel Pink's *A Whole New Mind.* See the Additional Resources section for more suggested reading.

4. Scott O. Lilienfeld and Hal Arkowitz, "Uncovering Brainscams." *Scientific American Mind,* February/March 2008 (pp. 80-81).

5. From *My Stroke Of Insight* by Jill Bolte Taylor, copyright © 2006 by Jill Bolte Taylor. Used by permission of Viking Penguin, a division of Penguin Group (USA) Inc. p. 140.

6.   Source: Institute of HeartMath website (www.HeartMath. com), *The Journal of Alternative and Complementary Medicine*, Volume 10, Number 2, 2004, pp. 325-336.

7.   "The $10,000-a-Month Psychic," by Tony Dokoupil, *Newsweek*, June 30, 2008 (www.newsweek.com).

8.   John Medina, *Brain Rules*, pp. 49-70.

9.   Michalko, Michael, *Cracking Creativity,* p.110.

10. Schulz, Mona Lisa, *Awakening Intuition*, p. 63.

11. Bench, Doug, *Mind Your Brain* Audio Program.

12. Medina, John, *Brain Rules,* pp. 80-81.

13. From *Rewiring The Corporate Brain* by Danah Zohar, copyright © 1997 by Danah Zohar. Used by permission of Berrett-Koehler Publishers, Inc. p. 82.

14. From *On Being Certain* by Robert Burton, M.D. Copyright © 2008 by Robert Burton, M.D. Published by St. Martin's Press. p. 150.

15. From *Martha: The Life And Work Of Martha Graham* by Agnes de Mille, copyright © 1991. Published by Random House, Inc.

16. Reprinted with the permission of The Free Press, a Division of Simon & Schuster, Inc., from *The Intention Experiment: Using Your Thoughts to Change Your Life and the World* by Lynne McTaggart. Copyright © 2007 by Lynne McTaggart. All rights reserved. p. xxi.

17. *Infinite Mind* by Valerie V. Hunt. Copyright © 1996 by Valerie V. Hunt. Published by Malibu Publishing.

18. From *Awakening Intuition* by Mona Lisa Schulz, copyright © 1998 by Mona Lisa Schulz. Used by permission of Harmony Books, a division of Random House, Inc. pp. 69-70.

19. *The Fifth Discipline* by Peter M. Senge. Copyright © 1990 by Peter M. Senge. Published by Doubleday. pp. 168-169.

20. From Wise Mind from http://www.dbtselfhelp.com, copyright © Lisa Dietz. Used by permission of Lisa Dietz.

21. From *My Stroke Of Insight* by Jill Bolte Taylor, copyright © 2006 by Jill Bolte Taylor. Used by permission of Viking Penguin, a division of Penguin Group (USA) Inc. p. 160.

22. "Are You an Intuitive Empath?" quiz, excerpted from "Positive Energy: Ten Extraordinary Perscriptions For Transforming Fatigue, Stress, And Fear Into Vibrance, Strength, And Love" and featured on http://www.drjudithorloff.com/Free-Articles/ Intuitive-Empath.htm by Judith Orloff, MD. Copyright © 2005 by Judith Orloff, M.D. Published by Harmony Books, a division of Random House.

23. From *Awakening Intuition* by Mona Lisa Schulz, copyright © 1998 by Mona Lisa Schulz. Published by Harmony Books, a division of Random House, Inc. pp. 332-333.

24. From *Awakening Intuition* by Mona Lisa Schulz, copyright © 1998 by Mona Lisa Schulz. Used by permission of Harmony Books, a division of Random House, Inc. p. 336.

25. Reprinted from: *The New Brain: How the Modern Age is Rewiring Your Mind* by Richard Restak. Copyright © 2003 by Richard Restak. Permission granted by Rodale, Inc., Emmaus, PA 18098. pp. 7-8.

26. Reprinted with the permission of The Free Press, a Division of Simon & Schuster, Inc., from *The Heart Of The Soul: Emotional Awareness* by Gary Zukav and Linda Francis. Copyright © 2001 by Gary Zukav and Linda Francis. All rights reserved. p. 13.

27. Reprinted with the permission of The Free Press, a Division of Simon & Schuster, Inc., from *The Heart Of The Soul: Emotional Awareness* by Gary Zukav and Linda Francis. Copyright © 2001 by Gary Zukav and Linda Francis. All rights reserved. p. 49.

28. *Loving What Is* by Byron Katie. Copyright © 2002 by Byron Kathleen Mitchell. Published by Harmony Books. p.15.

29. From *A New Earth: Awakening to Your Life's Purpose* by Eckhart Tolle, copyright © 2005 by Eckhart Tolle. All rights reserved. Published by Plume, a member of Penguin Group (USA) Inc. p. 147.

30. From *Evolve Your Brain* by Joe Dispenza, D.C., copyright © 2007 by Joe Dispenza, D.C. All rights reserved. Used by permission of Health Communications, Inc. p. 302.

31. From *Evolve Your Brain* by Joe Dispenza, D.C., copyright © 2007 by Joe Dispenza, D.C. All rights reserved. Used by permission of Health Communications, Inc. p. 313.

32. Both *Power Versus Force* by David R. Hawkins and *The Astonishing Power Of Emotions* by Esther and Jerry Hicks speak of the range of emotions, moving from more heavy or dense to light or higher vibrations. My grouping is based upon my interpretation of their work and my own experience.

33. *Drawing On The Right Side Of The Brain* by Betty Edwards. Copyright © 1999 by Betty Edwards. Published by Jeremy P. Tarcher/Putnam. pp. 3-9.

34. From *Electrophysiological Evidence of Intuition: Part 1. The Surprising Role of the Heart* by Dr. Rollin McCraty, director of research for the Institute of HeartMath, Mike Atkinson, and Raymond Trevor Bradley, Ph.D. © Copyright Institute of HeartMath Research Center. Published in *The Journal of Alternative and Complementary Medicine*, Volume 10, Number 1, 2004 pp. 133-143, © copyright Mary Ann Liebert, Inc.

35. From *Awakening Intuition* by Mona Lisa Schulz, copyright © 1998 by Mona Lisa Schulz. Used by permission of Harmony Books, a division of Random House, Inc. p. 116.

36. From *Power Versus Force: The Hidden Determinants of Human Behavior* by David R. Hawkins, copyright © 1995, 1998 by David R. Hawkins. Used by permission of Veritas Publishing, www.veritaspub.com. p. 10.

37. From *The Definitive Book Of Body Language* by Allan and Barbara Pease, copyright © 2004 by Allan and Barbara Pease. Published by Bantam Dell, a division of Random House, Inc. p. 11.

38. From *The Definitive Book Of Body Language* by Allan and Barbara Pease, copyright © 2004 by Allan and Barbara Pease. Published by Bantam Dell, a division of Random House, Inc. p. 10.

39. Brown, Harriet. "The Other Brain Also Deals With Many Woes." *The New York Times*, August 23, 2005. Retrieved September 4, 2008 from http://www.nytimes.com/2005/08/23/health/23gut.html. Also *The Other 90%* by Robert K. Cooper. Copyright © 2001 by Robert Cooper. Published by Three Rivers Press. pp. 15-16.

40. From *The Definitive Book Of Body Language* by Allan and Barbara Pease, copyright © 2004 by Allan and Barbara Pease. Published by Bantam Dell, a division of Random House, Inc. p. 253.

41. From *Power Versus Force: The Hidden Determinants of Human Behavior* by David R. Hawkins, copyright © 1995, 1998 by David R. Hawkins. Used by permission of Veritas Publishing, www.veritaspub.com. p. 112. Also, *Leadership And The New Science* by Margaret J. Wheatley. Copyright © 1994 by Margaret J. Wheatley. Published by Berrett-Koehler Publishers, Inc. pp. 50-56.

42. From *Electrophysiological Evidence of Intuition: Part 1. The Surprising Role of the Heart* by Dr. Rollin McCraty, director of research for the Institute of HeartMath, Mike Atkinson, and Raymond Trevor Bradley, Ph.D. © Copyright Institute of HeartMath Research Center. Published in *The Journal of Alternative and Complementary Medicine,* Volume 10, Number 1, 2004 P. 141, © copyright Mary Ann Liebert, Inc.

43. From *Electrophysiological Evidence of Intuition: Part 1. The Surprising Role of the Heart* by Dr. Rollin McCraty, director of research for the Institute of HeartMath, Mike Atkinson, and Raymond Trevor Bradley, Ph.D. © Copyright Institute of HeartMath Research Center. Published in *The Journal of Alternative and Complementary Medicine,* Volume 10, Number 1, 2004 P. 142, © copyright Mary Ann Liebert, Inc.

44. Reprinted with the permission of The Free Press, a Division of Simon & Schuster, Inc., from The *Intention Experiment: Using Your Thoughts to Change Your Life and the World* by Lynne McTaggart. Copyright © 2007 by Lynne McTaggart. All rights reserved. p. 181.

45. From the Global Consciousness Project website: http://
    noosphere.princeton.edu/. Roger Nelson, Director, Global
    Consciousness Project, copyright © 2008 by Roger Nelson for
    the Global Consciousness Project. Used by permission.

46. From *Edgar Mitchell's Epiphany* from http://www.noetic.org.
    Copyright © Institute of Noetic Sciences. Used by permission of
    the Institute of Noetic Sciences.

47. *The Tarot Handbook* by Angeles Arrien. Copyright © 1987 by
    Angeles Arrien. Published by Jeremy P. Tarcher/Putnam. p. 150.

48. From *The Scottish Himalayan Expedition* by W. H. Murray, ©
    1951 by W. H. Murray. Originally published by J.M. Dent &
    Sons Ltd.

49. *Secrets Of The Millionaire Mind* by T. Harv Eker. Copyright ©
    2005 by Harv Eker. Published by HarperCollins Publishers Inc.
    pp. 81-82.

50. From *The Scottish Himalayan Expedition* by W. H. Murray, ©
    1951 by W. H. Murray. Originally published by J.M. Dent &
    Sons Ltd.

51. "The Journey" from *Dream Work* by Mary Oliver. Copyright
    © 1986 by Mary Oliver. Used by permission of Grove/Atlantic,
    Inc.

52. From *Ten Poems To Change Your Life* by Roger Housden,
    copyright © 2001 by Roger Housden. Used by permission of
    Harmony Books, a division of Random House, Inc. pp. 11-12.

53. From *Ten Poems To Change Your Life* by Roger Housden,
    copyright © 2001 by Roger Housden. Used by permission of
    Harmony Books, a division of Random House, Inc. p. 12.

54. From Northern Sun Merchandising, copyright © 2004.
    www.northernsun.com.

Acknowledgments

When I finally decided to get serious about writing this book, everything fell into place. I have the talented team of professionals associated with the eWomenNetwork Publishing Group to thank for that:

* Jan King, the fearless leader of eWomenNetwork Publishing, who nudged me when needed and reminded me to celebrate my progress;

* Christine Frank of Christine Frank & Associates, who provided clarity and insight with her editing;

* Dawn Putney and Wendy Brookshire at True Self Publishing who brought this manuscript to life with outstanding cover design and interior design and layout; and

* Gail Richards of AuthorSmart for her in-depth programs and products designed to make writing and publishing a book something anyone can do.

The manuscript was strengthened immeasurably by the thoughtful feedback and suggestions from Patti DeNucci, Shari Pitts, and Metta Smith. They played a critical role in shaping the final book and will forever have my deep appreciation. And this book would still be "in process" without my assistant, Christy McDonald.

Stories bring concepts to life and inspire us. This book couldn't exist without the wonderful clients who shared their stories, allowed me to witness some of their powerful aha! moments, and inspired me with their dreams. I especially want to thank the men and women who graciously shared the details of their aha! moments and gave me permission to use their names: Greg Davis, Bart Emken, Diane Graden, Mary Ann Halpin, and Barbara Metzger. And to Sara Blakely whose story is a testament to the power of aha! moments, thank you for spreading the word about what trusting your gut can do for you.

With deep gratitude, I also want to thank my friends and family for their faith in me, even when they had no clue what the journey over the past eight years was about (Dad, I'm especially talking about you). Special thanks for their unwavering support go to Jim and Kristy Tiampo, who offered a helping hand when I needed it most. And Janet O'Leary, Melinda Gray, Darlene LaBree, Chris Seitter, Connie Brubaker, Julie Tereshchuk, Monica Benoit-Beatty, Reneé Peterson Trudeau, Andy Choquette, and Mike Doughty, who offered encouragement at critical points in the process. And finally, my gratitude goes to the number one source of all of my smiles and laughter each day: Forest. I can't thank you enough for helping me stay sane during this process.

Index